ULTIMATE LANDSCAPE DESIGN

teNeues

ULTIMATE LANDSCAPE DESIGN

Editor in chief: Paco Asensio

Project coordination and texts: Alejandro Bahamón

Editorial Assistant: Eva Raventós

Research: Alex Campello

Art director: Mireia Casanovas Soley

Layout: Cristina Granero Navarro

Copy editing: Alessandro Orsi

English translation: Matthew C. Conell, Michael Brunelle

German translation: Susanne Engler

French translation: Michel Ficerai/Lingo Sense

Italian translation: Maurizio Siliato

Produced by Loft Publications
www.loftpublications.com

Published by teNeues Publishing Group

teNeues Publishing Company
16 West 22nd Street, New York, NY 10010, USA
Tel.: 001-212-627-9090, Fax: 001-212-627-9511

teNeues Book Division
Kaistraße 18, 40221 Düsseldorf, Germany
Tel.: 0049-(0)211-994597-0, Fax: 0049-(0)211-994597-40

teNeues Publishing UK Ltd.
P.O. Box 402, West Byfleet, KT14 7ZF, Great Britain
Tel.: 0044-1932-403509, Fax: 0044-1932-403514

teNeues France S.A.R.L.
4, rue de Valence, 75005 Paris, France
Tel.: 0033-1-55 76 62 05, Fax: 0033-1-55 76 64 19

teNeues Iberica S.L.
Pso. Juan de la Encina 2-48, Urb. Club de Campo
28700 S.S.R.R., Madrid, Spain
Tel./Fax: 0034-91-65 95 876

www.teneues.com
© 2005 teNeues Verlag GmbH + Co. KG, Kempen

ISBN-10: 3-8327-9057-8
ISBN-13: 978-3-8327-9057-8

Editorial project: 2005 **LOFT** Publications
Via Laietana 32, 4º Of. 92
08003 Barcelona, Spain
Tel.: 0034 932 688 088
Fax: 0034 932 687 073

e-mail: loft@loftpublications.com
www.loftpublications.com

Printed by: Anman Gràfiques del Vallès, Spain
www.anman.com
anman@anman.com
2005

Bibliographic information published by
Die Deutsche Bibliothek.
Die Deutsche Bibliothek lists this publication
in the Deutsche Nationalbibliografie;
detailed bibliographic data is available
in the Internet at http://dnb.ddb.de

Content

In recent years, we have witnessed a true revolution in the way that landscapes are designed and understood. What in the past was considered part of the job performed by architects or civil engineers has come to be considered an independent discipline that makes use of concepts from architecture, urban design, biology, and contemporary art.

Abstraction, as applied to landscape design, was an idea that was completely foreign to contemporary art until the beginning of the 20th century. The International Exposition of the Decorative and Industrial Arts celebrated in Paris in 1925 is considered to be the key that opened the door to Modernism in landscape architecture. In fact, during the period between the world wars, concepts from other disciplines were being borrowed to outline the first theories, which would later be fully developed (especially by young California architects and designers during the forties and fifties) and be referred to as the "architectural garden".

During the 1960's, the main objective of the environmental artists was to take art out of galleries. What later became known as Land Art enabled the blurring of the lines between art, environment, and landscape design, which by then was already considered an independent discipline, especially in the United States.

The social, political, and economic developments of the subsequent decades contributed key concepts to the discipline. Acid rain and the greenhouse effect sparked an ecological conscience during the 1970's, while the economic development in Asia and the political transformations in Eastern Europe of the 1980's emphasized the important role of public space.

The landscape is constantly transformed and renewed and concepts such as sustainable development, globalization, mass tourism, and communication directly affect its design. Both the latest political events as well as the recent technological advances have a clear influence on the way we understand contemporary landscape and its role in the public spaces of cities. Their cultural connotations and reduced scale—if compared with projects in rural environments—have great compositional, functional, and conceptual power.

This book concentrates on recent urban projects in a variety of locations that are unique in their audacity in resolving a wide range of conditioning factors. The book, which is divided into five chapters that summarize the most characteristic types—plazas, parks, river banks, gardens, and festivals—offers many examples of the ways contemporary landscape is understood and designed, and it is at the same time a testimonial document, recognizing that this discipline is changing as much as the landscape itself.

Introduction

In den letzten Jahren hat eine wahre Revolution in der Art und Weise stattgefunden, wie man Landschaft versteht und gestaltet. Was man früher als eine Arbeit verstand, die parallel von Architekten oder Bauingenieuren durchgeführt wurde, hat sich mit der Zeit zu einem eigenen Bereich entwickelt und ist heute eine unabhängige Disziplin, die Konzepte der Architektur, der Stadtgestaltung, der Biologie und der zeitgenössischen Kunst verwendet.

Die Abstraktion, die auf die Landschaftsgestaltung angewandt wird, war bis zum Anfang des 20. Jh. ein Konzept, das nichts mit den Schönen Künsten gemeinsam hatte. Man kann heute bestätigen, dass die Internationale Ausstellung der Dekorativen und Industriellen Künste in Paris 1925 der Schlüssel war, der dem Modernismus die Tür zur Landschaftsarchitektur geöffnet hat. In der Zeit zwischen den Weltkriegen kamen allmählich Konzepte aus anderen Disziplinen hinzu, mit deren Hilfe man eine erste Theorie skizzieren konnte, die bald darauf weiterentwickelt wurde, vor allem von jungen, kalifornischen Architekten und Gestaltern in den Vierziger- und Fünfzigerjahren des 20. Jh. So entstand die Vorstellung vom „architektonischen Garten".

In den Sechzigerjahren war es das Hauptziel der Umweltkünstler, die Kunst aus den Galerien herauszuholen. Diese Bewegung, die später als Land Art bekannt wurde, verwischte die Grenzen zwischen Kunst, Umgebung und Gestaltung der Landschafts, die bis zu jener Zeit als unabhängige Disziplinen betrachtet wurden, bei deren Entwicklung die Vereinigten Staaten eine führende Stellung einnahmen.

Die sozialen, politischen und wirtschaftlichen Ereignisse der darauf folgenden Jahrzehnte führten dazu, dass verschiedene Schlüsselkonzepte in diese Disziplin integriert wurden. Der saure Regen und der Treibhauseffekt ließen in den Siebzigerjahren ein ökologisches Bewusstsein entstehen, während das Wirtschaftswachstum in

Asien und die politischen Veränderungen im Osten Europas in den Achtzigerjahren die Bedeutung des öffentlichen Raumes als Bühne für das Weltgeschehen deutlich werden ließ.

Die Landschaft wird ständig umgestaltet und erneuert und Konzepte wie umweltgerechte Entwicklung, Globalisierung, Massentourismus oder Kommunikation wirken sich direkt auf die Gestaltung aus. Sowohl die politischen Ereignisse als auch der technologische Fortschritt beeinflussen erkennbar die Art und Weise, wie zeitgenössische Landschaft und Eingriffe in die öffentlichen Räume der Städte verstanden werden. Diese Räume besitzen kulturelle Konnotationen und sind oft sehr klein, wenn man sie mit Projekten in ländlicher Umgebung vergleicht, so dass sie eine große gestalterische, funktionelle und konzeptuelle Last tragen.

Dieses Buch konzentriert sich auf neue Projekte in Städten an sehr verschiedenen Standorten, bei denen man sich zu einer gewagten Lösung für ein breites Spektrum an Varanssetzungen entschlossen hat. Der Band unterteilt sich in fünf Kapitel, die die wichtigsten Projekttypen zusammenfassen: Plätze, Parks, Ufer, Gärten und Festivals. So erhält man einen ausgezeichneten Überblick über neue Tendenzen und Verständnis von zeitgenössischer Gestaltung der Landschaft innerhalb ihrer städtischen Umgebung, sowie eine Dokumentation, die zeigt, dass sich diese Disziplin genauso verändert wie die Landschaft selbst.

Einleitung

Ces dernières années ont permis d'assister à une véritable révolution dans la manière d'appréhender et de concevoir le paysage. Ce qui, auparavant, était considéré comme un travail parallèle réalisé par des architectes et ingénieurs civils, s'est peu à peu consolidé, de nos jours, comme une discipline indépendante recourant aux concepts de l'architecture, du design urbain, de la biologie et de l'art contemporain.

L'abstraction, appliquée au design de paysage, a été un concept complètement étranger aux Beaux-arts jusqu'à l'orée du XXème siècle. L'on a pu affirmer que l'Exposition internationale des arts décoratifs et industriels, célébrée à Paris en 1925, fut la clé ouvrant la porte du modernisme dans l'architecture paysagiste. De fait, lors de l'entre-deux guerres, des concepts d'autres disciplines ont commencé à filtrer, permettant d'ébaucher une première théorie qui serait par la suite amplement développée – principalement par de jeunes architectes et créateurs californiens des années 1940 et 1950 – pour déboucher sur la notion de « jardin architectural ».

Au cours des années 1960, les artistes environnementaux avaient pour objectif principal de tirer parti des galeries. Ce qui serait ensuite connu comme le « Land Art » sut, alors, effacer les frontières entre l'art, l'environnement et le paysagisme, déjà considéré comme une discipline indépendante dont les États-Unis stimulaient le développement.

Les événements sociaux, politiques et économiques des décennies suivantes ont incorporé les concepts clés de la discipline : les pluies acides et l'effet de serre ont réveillé, dans les années 1970, une conscience écologique alors que la croissance économique asiatique et les évolutions politiques de l'Europe de l'Est des années 1980 ont souligné l'importance d'offrir une chaleur scénique à l'espace public.

Le paysage est transformé et rénové constamment et des concepts comme le développement durable, la globalisation, le tourisme de masse ou la communication affectent directement son design. Les plus récents événements politiques tout comme les ultimes avancées technologiques influencent clairement la façon de comprendre le paysage contemporain et les interventions dans l'espace public des villes, de par leurs connotations culturelles et une échelle réduite – par comparaison avec les projets dans un cadre rural – possèdent un forte charge compositionnelle, fonctionnelle et conceptuelle.

Cet ouvrage se centre sur les projets urbains récents se détachant par leur audace dans la réso-lution d'une ample palette de conditions et couvrant une grande diversité d'emplacements. Organisé en cinq chapitres qui résument les typologies les plus caractéristiques – places, parcs, rives, jardins et festivals – cet ouvrage offre un parcours complet de la manière de comprendre et de concevoir le paysage urbain contemporain et se convertit, à son tour, en un document témoin, enseignant que cette discipline est aussi changeante que le paysage lui-même.

Introduction

En los últimos años se ha asistido a una verdadera revolución en la manera de entender y diseñar el paisaje. Lo que antes se consideraba una labor paralela desempeñada por arquitectos o ingenieros civiles se ha ido consolidando y es, hoy en día, una disciplina independiente que utiliza conceptos de la arquitectura, del diseño urbano, de la biología y del arte contemporáneo.

La abstracción, aplicada al diseño del paisaje, ha sido un concepto completamente ajeno a las bellas artes hasta comienzos del siglo XX. Se puede afirmar que la Exposición Internacional de Artes Decorativas e Industriales, celebrada en París en 1925, fue la llave que abrió la puerta al modernismo en la arquitectura del paisaje. De hecho, en el período de entreguerras comienzan a filtrarse conceptos de otras disciplinas que permiten esbozar una primera teoría que será luego ampliamente desarrollada (principalmente por jóvenes arquitectos y diseñadores californianos durante los años cuarenta y cincuenta) y que desembocará en la noción de "jardín arquitectónico".

En los años sesenta, el objetivo principal de los artistas medioambientales fue sacar el arte de las galerías; lo que luego se conoció como Land Art logró desdibujar las barreras entre arte, entorno y diseño del paisaje, que, por aquel entonces, ya se consideraba una disciplina independiente cuyo desarrollo lideraba Estados Unidos.

Los acontecimientos sociales, políticos y económicos de los decenios posteriores incorporaron conceptos claves a la disciplina: la lluvia ácida y el efecto invernadero despertaron, durante los años setenta, una con-

ciencia ecológica, mientras que el crecimiento económico en Asia y las transformaciones políti-
cas del este europeo en los años ochenta destacaron la importancia de proporcionar al espacio
público una calidad escénica.

El paisaje es transformado y renovado constantemente y conceptos como desarrollo sostenible,
globalización, turismo de masas o comunicación afectan directamente a su diseño. Tanto los
últimos acontecimientos políticos como los recientes avances tecnológicos tienen una clara
influencia en la manera de entender el paisaje contemporáneo y las intervenciones en el espacio público de las ciudades, por sus connotaciones culturales y por su escala reducida –si se com-
para con proyectos en entornos rurales–, poseen una gran carga compositiva, funcional y conceptual.

Este libro se centra en proyectos urbanos recientes que destacan por su audacia en la resolución
de un amplio abanico de condicionantes y abarcan una gran variedad de localizaciones.
Organizado en cinco capítulos que resumen las tipologías más características –plazas, parques,
orillas, jardines y festivales– este volumen ofrece un amplio recorrido por la manera de entender y diseñar el paisaje urbano contemporáneo y se convierte, a su vez, en documento testimonial, a sabiendas de que esta disciplina es tan cambiante como el paisaje mismo.

Introducción

Negli ultimi anni abbiamo assistito a una vera e propria rivoluzione nel modo di intendere e progettare il paesaggio. Ciò che prima veniva considerato un lavoro parallelo svolto da architetti o da ingegneri civili si è man mano consolidato, ed è attualmente, una disciplina indipendente che utilizza concetti di architettura, progettazione urbanistica, biologia ed arte contemporanea.

L'astrazione, applicata alla progettazione paesaggistica è stata un concetto completamente estraneo al mondo delle belle arti fino all'inizio del XX secolo. Si può affermare che l'Esposizione Internazionale di Arti Decorative e Industriali, tenutasi a Parigi nel 1925, sia stata la chiave che ha aperto le porte al modernismo nell'architettura del paesaggio. Di fatto, nel periodo tra le due guerre si comincia ad assorbire concetti propri di altre discipline che consentono di abbozzare una prima teoria che verrà poi sviluppata più ampiamente (soprattutto da giovani architetti e designer californiani degli anni quaranta e cinquanta) e che sfocerà nella nozione di "giardino architettonico".

Negli anni sessanta, l'obiettivo principale degli artisti ambientali fu quello di portare l'arte fuori dalle gallerie; ciò che si conobbe come Land Art riuscì a far scomparire le barriere tra arte, ambiente e progettazione del paesaggio, che già all'epoca, veniva considerata una disciplina indipendente, promossa soprattutto da artisti americani.

Gli eventi sociali, politici ed economici dei decenni posteriori hanno favorito l'integrazione di concetti chiave in questa disciplina: negli anni settanta, la pioggia acida e l'effetto serra hanno risvegliato la coscienza ecologica, mentre la crescita economica dell'Asia e le trasformazioni politiche dell'est europeo negli anni ottanta hanno evidenziato l'importanza di dare allo spazio pubblico una qualità scenica.

Il paesaggio viene trasformato e rinnovato costantemente e concetti quali sviluppo sostenibile, globalizzazione, turismo di massa o comunicazione incidono direttamente sulla sua progettazione. Sia gli ultimi eventi politici che i recenti progressi in campo tecnologico hanno una forte influenza sul modo di intendere il paesaggio contemporaneo. Di conseguenza, gli interventi negli spazi pubblici delle città, per via delle loro connotazioni culturali e per la loro scala ridotta – se si paragonano a progetti in ambienti rurali – possiedono un'enorme carica compositiva, funzionale e concettuale.

Questo libro si concentra principalmente su progetti urbani recenti, ubicati in località e paesi diversi, che hanno saputo superare con audacia un'ampia varietà di condizionamenti. Il volume, diviso in cinque capitoli che riassumono le tipologie più caratteristiche – piazze, parchi, sponde, giardini e festival – ripercorre il modo di intendere e progettare il paesaggio urbano contemporaneo, trasformandosi a sua volta, in un documento testimoniale che illustra i cambiamenti di questa disciplina, cangiante come il paesaggio stesso.

Introduzione

Parks · Parks · Parcs · Parques · Parchi

Rosa Grena Kliass

Parque da Juventude

Location: São Paulo, Brazil **Completion Year:** 2004 **Photos:** © Nelson Kon

The lot, previously occupied by a penitentiary, has been turned into a large city park. The old pavilions were adapted for housing cultural, educational, and health centers. A long walk lined with native trees acts as the center that the entire complex revolves around.

Dieses Grundstück, auf dem sich vorher eine Strafanstalt befand, wurde zu einem großen Stadtpark umgestaltet. Die alten Pavillons wurden zu Zentren für Kultur, Erziehung und Gesundheit umgebaut. Die lange Allee, an der einheimische Bäume gepflanzt wurden, dient als Achse, um die herum sich der gesamte Park organisiert.

Le terrain, auparavant occupé par un établissement pénitentiaire, a été converti en un vaste parc métropolitain. Les anciens pavillons ont été adaptés pour héberger des centres culturels, éducatifs et de santé. Une grande promenade plantée d'arbres d'essences autochtones constitue l'axe autour duquel l'ensemble s'organise.

El solar que antes ocupaba un establecimiento penitenciario ha sido convertido en un amplio parque metropolitano. Los antiguos pabellones se han adaptado para albergar centros culturales, educativos y de salud. Una larga alameda donde han sido plantados árboles de especies autóctonas es el eje alrededor del cual se organiza todo el conjunto.

Il terreno occupato originariamente da un centro penitenziario è stato trasformato in un vasto parco metropolitano. Gli antichi padiglioni sono stati adattati per ospitare centri culturali, educativi e sanitari. Un lungo viale dove sono stati piantati alberi di specie autoctone costituisce l'asse principale attorno a cui si struttura tutto l'insieme.

General Plan

Stairs Detail

General Sections

Pavilion Detail

EMBT Arquitectes Associats

Parc de Diagonal Mar

Location: Barcelona, Spain Completion Year: 2002 Photos: © Roger Casas

This park's large size is accentuated by its relationship with the Avenida Diagonal, Taulat Street, and the direct connection with the Barcelona beach. The park is based on a central axis from which different roads radiate, like the branches of a tree, extending in every direction.

Die Größe dieses Parks wird durch seine Beziehung zur Avenida Diagonal, zur Taulat-Straße und die direkte Verbindung zum Strand von Barcelona noch unterstrichen. Der Park wird von einer zentralen Achse strukturiert, von der Wege, die sich in verschiedene Richtungen ausbreiten, wie die Zweige eines Baumes abgehen.

Les amples proportions du parc sont accentuées par sa relation avec l'avenue Diagonal, la rue Taulat et la connexion directe avec la plage de Barcelone. Le parc se structure autour d'un axe central duquel bourgeonnent des chemins qui, comme les branches d'un arbre, s'étendent dans tous les sens.

Las grandes proporciones del parque son acentuadas por su relación con la Avenida Diagonal, la calle Taulat y la conexión directa con la playa de Barcelona. El parque se estructura alrededor de un eje central del que brotan caminos que, como ramas de árbol, se extienden en diferentes sentidos.

Le grandi proporzioni del parco vengono accentuate dal rapporto con la Avenida Diagonal, la via Taulat e il collegamento diretto con la spiaggia di Barcellona. Il parco si struttura attorno ad un asse centrale da cui si diramano sentieri che, al pari delle radici di un albero, si estendono in varie direzioni.

General Plan

Germán del Sol

Geometrical Thermal Springs

Location: Villarrica National Park, Chile Completion Year: 2003 Photos: © Guy Wemborne

The project consisted of renovating some natural hot water springs for public use. Twenty pools were dug out along the fissure for bathing, which can be accessed by ramps and passageways. The overall composition is based on overlaying light elements, maintaining great respect for the delicate landscape.

Innerhalb dieses Projektes sollten Thermalquellen als Heilbad gestaltet werden. Dazu wurden am Wasserlauf entlang zwanzig Schwimmbecken zum Baden ausgehoben, die man über Laufstege und Zugangsrampen erreicht. Die Gesamtkomposition besteht aus leichten, übereinander gelagerten Elementen, die sich gut in die zerbrechlich wirkende Landschaft einfügen.

Le projet vise à habiliter des sources thermales d'eau chaude à un usage public ; 20 piscines ont été creusées au long du ravin pour la baignade. Elles sont accessibles par des passerelles et des rampes d'accès. La composition générale, fondée sur des éléments légers superposés, respecte au maximum la fragilité du paysage.

El proyecto consiste en habilitar unas fuentes termales de agua caliente para uso público; a lo largo de la quebrada se cavaron 20 pozas para bañarse a las que se accede por medio de pasarelas y rampas de acceso. La composición general, que se basa en elementos ligeros que se superponen, respeta al máximo el frágil paisaje.

Il progetto consisteva nell'adibire delle sorgenti termali di acqua calda ad uso pubblico; lungo la fenditura sono state scavate 20 pozze dove bagnarsi e alle quali si accede mediante passerelle e apposite rampe. La composizione generale, che si basa su elementi leggeri sovrapposti, rispetta al massimo il fragile paesaggio.

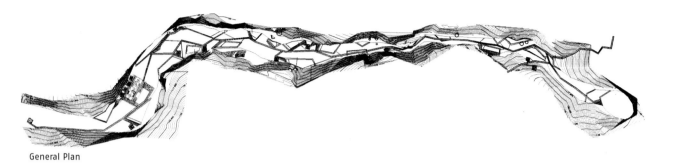

General Plan

Path Plan

Raderschall Landschaftsarchitekten

MFO Park

Location: Zurich, Switzerland **Completion Year:** 2002 **Photos:** © Markus Fierz

A steel structure 300 feet long and 50 feet tall, which was designed to be covered by climbing plants over time, provides an area of shade where one can relax, in addition to offering a sufficiently large space to organize outdoor events. Staircases and platforms give the visitor a privileged view over the site.

Eine fast 100 m lange und 15 m hohe Stahlstruktur, die im Laufe der Zeit von Pflanzen überwachsen werden soll, sorgt für schattige Bereiche, in denen man sich entspannen kann und die tusätzlich als Veranstaltungsort im Freien dienen. Die Treppen und Plattformen bilden Aussichtspunkte.

Une structure d'acier de presque 100 m de long sur 15 m de haut, pensée pour se couvrir de végéta- tion, avec le temps, offre une zone ombragée où se détendre ainsi qu'un espace suffisant pour orga- niser des spectacles à l'air libre. Escaliers et plateformes servent de points de vue.

Una estructura de acero de casi 100 m de largo y 15 m de alto, pensada para que, con el tiempo, se cubra de vegetación, proporciona una zona de sombra donde relajarse y ofrece el espacio suficiente para organizar espectáculos al aire libre. Escaleras y plataformas sirven de miradores.

Una struttura in acciaio lunga quasi 100 m e alta 15, pensata affinché, col tempo, si possa coprire di vegetazione, offre una zona d'ombra dove rilassarsi e lo spazio sufficiente per organizzare spettacoli all'aperto. Scale e piattaforme servono da belvedere.

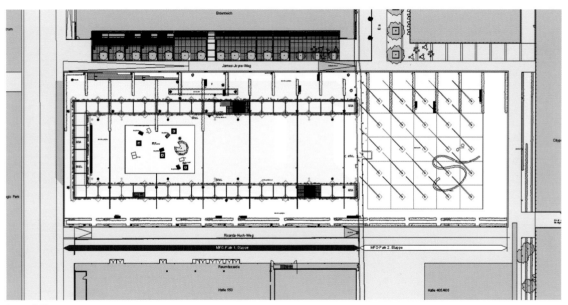

General Plan

Janet Rosenberg & Associates

Barrel Warehouse Park

Location: Waterloo, Canada Completion Year: 2001 Photos: © Neil Fox

What was originally an industrial area of Waterloo was transformed into a residential neighborhood, through the renovation of distillery buildings for use as homes. The design of this new park displays a mixture of traditional and contemporary elements, and makes clear references to industrial buildings in the layout of the plantings, sculptures, and furniture.

Ein ehemaliges Industriegebiet in Waterloo wurch durch die Umnutzung der Brennerei in ein Wohnviertel umgestaltet. Das Design dieses neuen Parks mischt traditionelle mit zeitgenössischen Elementen und klaren Anspielungen auf die industrielle Vergangenheit, sowohl in der Anordnung der Pflanzen als auch der der Skulpturen und des Mobiliars.

Une ancienne zone industrielle de Waterloo a été convertie en zone résidentielle en transformant de vieilles distilleries en logements. Le design du nouveau parc présente un mélange d'éléments traditionnels et contemporains aux références industrielles claires, tant pour la disposition des éléments végétaux que pour les sculptures et le mobilier.

Una antigua zona industrial de Waterloo ha sido convertida en zona residencial transformando antiguas destilerías en viviendas. El diseño del nuevo parque presenta una mezcla de elementos tradicionales y contemporáneos con claros referentes industriales, tanto en la disposición de los elementos vegetales como en las esculturas y en el mobiliario.

Una vecchia zona industriale di Waterloo è stata trasformata in zona residenziale tramutando le antiche distillerie in abitazioni. Il disegno del nuovo parco presenta una mescolanza di elementi tradizionali e contemporanei con chiari riferimenti industriali, sia nella disposizione degli elementi vegetali che nelle sculture e nell'arredo urbano.

Reynir Vilhjálmsson/Landslag

Protection Structures

Location: Siglufjordur, Iceland **Completion Year:** 2000 **Photos:** © Steingrimur Kristinsson, Thrainn Hauksson

After the avalanches of 1995, the Icelandic government pushed through the creation of containment barriers to protect the residents of this village. The two crests of these protective structures gently meld into the landscape and the urban environment of the village, whose inhabitants have come to use them as an observatory.

Nach den Lawinen im Jahr 1995 ließ die isländische Regierung Lawinendämme errichten, um den Ort zu schützen. Die beiden Kämme der Schutzwälle integrieren sich sanft in die Landschaft und in die Umgebung des Dorfes, dessen Einwohner sie mittlerweile als Observatorium benutzen.

Suite aux avalanches de 1995, le Gouvernement islandais a promu la création de barrières pour protéger la population. Les deux crêtes des structures de protection s'intègrent en douceur dans le paysage et l'environnement urbain du village, finissant par les accepter en tant que points d'observation.

Tras los aludes de 1995, el gobierno islandés promovió la creación de barreras para proteger a la población. Las dos crestas de las estructuras protectoras se integran suavemente en el paisaje y en el entorno urbano del pueblo, que ha acabado adoptándolas como observatorio.

In seguito alle valanghe del 1995, il governo islandese promosse la creazione di barriere per proteggere la popolazione. Le due creste delle strutture di protezione si integrano armoniosamente nel paesaggio e contesto urbano del paese, che ha finito per utilizzarle come osservatorio.

General View

Sketches

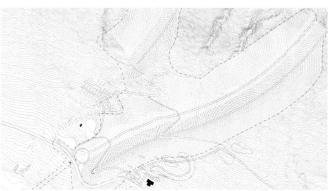

General Plan

ASPECT Landscape Architecture

Foshan City Park and Waterfront Park

Collaborators: IAPA

Location: Foshan, China Completion Year: 2006 Photos: © Aspect, IAPA

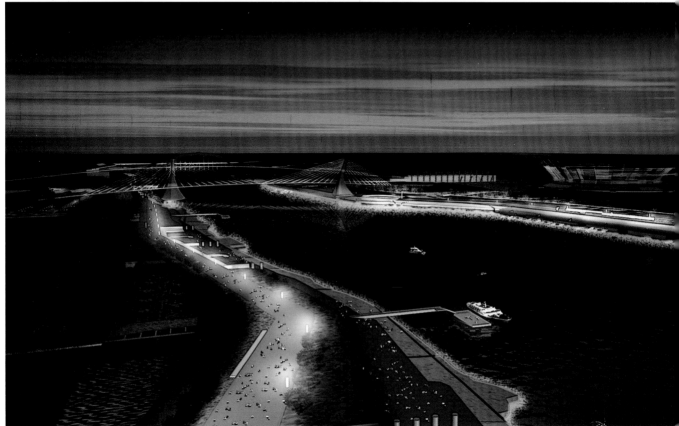

City Park and Waterfront Park in Foshan, in Southern China, form one of the largest metropolitan parks in existence. The design integrates the most sophisticated techniques for sustainable development and a large athletic center within the framework of contemporary design.

Der City Park und der Waterfront Park in Foshan im Süden Chinas bilden einen der größten Stadtparks weltweit. Bei dieser Planung wurden die innovativsten Techniken für nachhaltige Entwicklung eingesetzt und ein großer Komplex von Sportanlagen in zeitgenössischem Design geschaffen.

Le City Park et le Waterfront Park, à Foshan, au sud de la Chine, forment l'un des plus grands parcs métropolitains du monde. Le projet intègre les techniques les plus sophistiquées de développement durable et un vaste ensemble d'équipements sportifs dans le cadre d'un design contemporain.

El City Park y el Waterfront Park, en Foshan, al sur de China, forman uno de los más grandes parques metropolitanos que existen. El proyecto integra las más sofisticadas técnicas de desarrollo sostenible y un vasto complejo de equipamientos deportivos en un marco de diseño contemporáneo.

A Foshan, nel sud della Cina, il City Park e il Waterfront Park, formano uno dei più grandi parchi metropolitani esistenti attualmente. Il progetto integra le più sofisticate tecniche di sviluppo sostenibile e una grande varietà di infrastrutture sportive in una cornice dalle linee contemporanee.

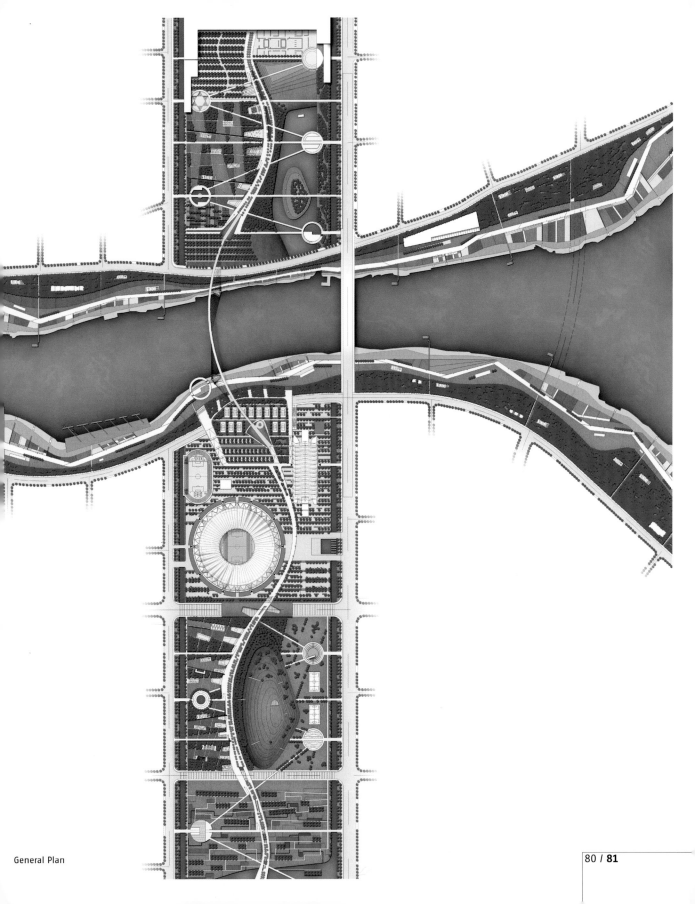

RCR Arquitectes

Tussols–Basil Track and Field Stadium

Location: Olot, Spain **Completion Year:** 2002 **Photos:** © Eugeni Pons

This running track is located in a clearing in a white oak forest whose impressive presence forms an integral part of the project's design. The arrangement of the trees was used to add various geometric designs to this athletic space.

Dieser Sportplatz befindet sich auf einer Lichtung in einem Wald aus Weißeichen, deren beeindruckendes Aussehen ein wichtiges Gestaltungselement ist. Die Anordnung der Bäume wurden benutzt, um bei diesem Sportplatz verschiedene geometrische Muster zu betonen.

Cette piste d'athlétisme se situe dans la clairière d'un bois de chênes blancs, dont la présence impressionnante est partie intégrante du design du projet. La disposition des arbres a été utilisée pour conférer différentes géométries à cet espace sportif.

Esta pista de atletismo se ubica en el claro de un bosque de robles albar, cuya impresionante presencia es parte integral del diseño del proyecto. La disposición de los árboles se ha utilizado para conferir diferentes geometrías a este espacio deportivo.

Questa pista di atletica sorge nella radura di un bosco di rovere bianco, e la sua imponente presenza è parte integrale del disegno del progetto. La disposizione degli alberi è stata studiata in modo tale da conferire diverse geometrie a questo spazio sportivo.

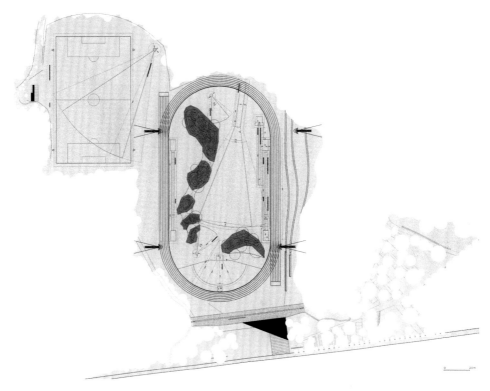

General Plan

Sketches

Fauteux et Associés

Parc des Locomotives

Location: Montreal, Canada **Completion Year:** 2004 **Photos:** © Guy Tremblay

The large infrastructures of this industrial neighborhood, which was Canada's most important production center in the 20th century, have been remodeled to create a new area for mixed use. The contemporary design of the park evokes the long gone industrial elements.

Die große Infrastruktur dieses Industriegebietes, das das wichtigste Produktionszentrum Kanadas im 20. Jh. war, wurde zu einer Zone mit gemischter Nutzung umgestaltet. Der Park spielt in zeitgenössischer Sprache auf die verschwundenen, industriellen Elemente an.

Les grandes infrastructures de ce quartier industriel, qui fut le centre de production le plus important du Canada au XXème siècle, ont été reconverties pour créer une nouvelle zone à usage mixte. Le parc évoque, par un langage contemporain, les éléments industriels disparus.

Las grandes infraestructuras de este barrio industrial, que fue el centro de producción más importante de Canadá en el siglo XX, se han reconvertido para crear una nueva zona de uso mixto. El parque evoca, mediante un lenguaje contemporáneo, los elementos industriales desaparecidos.

Le grandi infrastrutture di questo quartiere industriale, che è stato il centro di produzione più importante del Canada nel XX secolo, sono state riconvertite per creare una zona nuova ad uso misto. Il parco evoca, mediante un linguaggio contemporaneo, gli elementi industriali ormai scomparsi.

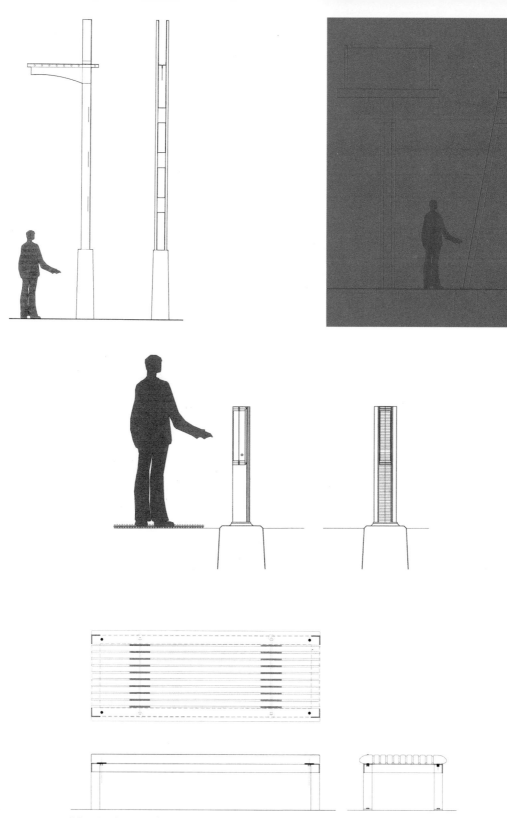

Urban Furniture Drawings

Paolo L. Bürgi

Cardada Intervention

Location: Locarno, Switzerland **Completion Year:** 2001 **Photos:** © Jean Michel Landecy

This project traces a path that leads visitors through an extremely beautiful yet fragile landscape. Nature is unveiled bit by bit along an itinerary that culminates in an impressive overlook.

Der Besucher wird hier durch eine wunderschöne und gleichzeitig sehr zerbrechliche Landschaft geführt. Die Natur zeigt sich ganz allmählich, wenn man der Strecke folgt, die an einem beeindrucken-den Aussichtspunkt endet.

Le projet trace un parcours conduisant les visiteurs dans un paysage à la beauté extrême et, en même temps, d'une grande fragilité. La nature se découvre peu à peu au fil de l'itinéraire qui culmine par un impressionnant point de vue.

El proyecto traza un recorrido que conduce a los visitantes por un paisaje de extrema belleza y, al mismo tiempo, de gran fragilidad. La naturaleza se muestra poco a poco a lo largo de un itinerario que culmina en un impresionante mirador.

Il progetto traccia un percorso che conduce i visitatori in un paesaggio di estrema bellezza e allo stes-so tempo di grande fragilità. La natura si mostra poco a poco lungo un itinerario che culmina in un meraviglioso belvedere.

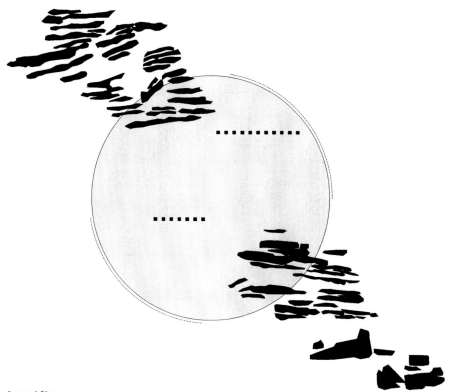

General Plan

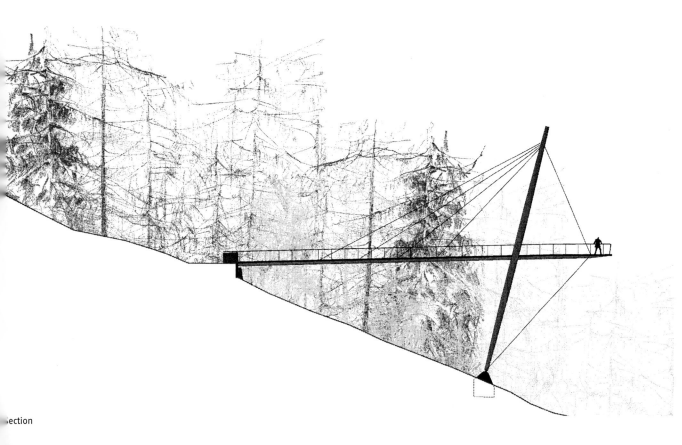

Section

Obras architectes

Parc de la Ereta

Location: Alicante, Spain **Completion Year:** 2004 **Photos:** © Obras architects

The park covers a large area surrounded by the old section of Alicante, the old castle above the cliff, and the bay on the ocean side. The location and its size determined the character of the design, which was planned as a space that highlights the surrounding elements.

Dieser Park befindet sich auf einer weiten Fläche, die von der Altstadt von Alicante, der alten Burg über den Felsen und der Bucht, die sich zum Meer öffnet, umgeben ist. Aufgrund seiner Lage und seiner Ausmaße wurde ein öffentlicher Raum geschaffen, der als Verbindungsglied zwischen den umgebenden Elementen dient.

Le parc s'étend sur une vaste superficie entourée par le centre ancien d'Alicante, la falaise dominée par l'antique château et la baie scrutant la mer. Sa situation et ses dimensions ont déterminé le caractère du projet, qui se propose comme un espace articulant les éléments environnants.

El parque se extiende por una amplia superficie rodeada por el casco antiguo de Alicante, el acantilado dominado por el antiguo castillo y la bahía que mira al mar. Su situación y sus dimensiones determinaron el carácter del proyecto que se propone como un espacio que articula los elementos circundantes.

Il parco si estende lungo un'ampia superficie circondata dal centro storico di Alicante, dalla falesia dominata dall'antico castello e la baia che guarda verso il mare. La sua ubicazione e le sue dimensioni hanno determinato il carattere del progetto che si propone come uno spazio che articola gli elementi circostanti.

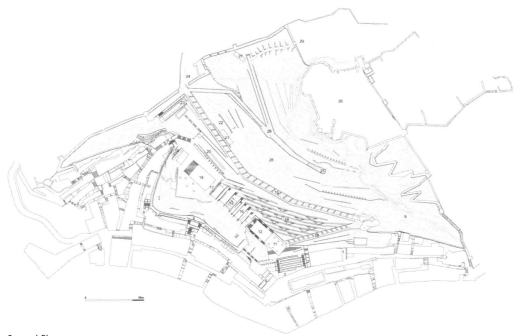

General Plan

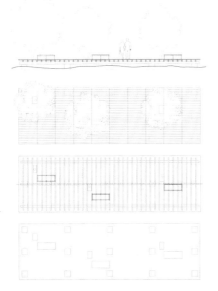

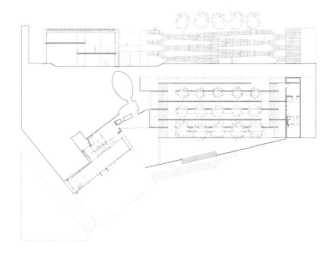

Shelter Structure Drawings

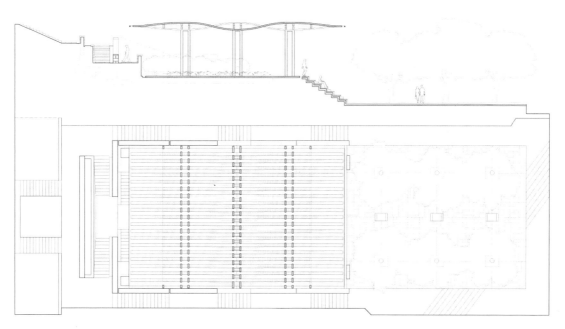

Pavilion Drawings

Germán del Sol

Puritama Springs

Location: San Pedro de Atacama, Chile **Completion Year:** 2000 **Photos:** © Guy Wemborne

The challenge of this project was creating public bathing areas without disturbing the natural environment of the river in this wide valley. The wooden dock allows the water to be enjoyed without having to walk on the grass that covers the banks.

In diesem großen Tal sollten öffentliche Badeanstalten entstehen, ohne dass dabei die natürliche Umgebung des Flusses negativ beeinflusst wird. Von dem Holzsteg aus kann man ins Wasser gehen, ohne über die Uferwiese laufen zu müssen.

Cette vaste vallée lance le défi de projeter des bains publics affectant au minimum le cadre naturel de la rivière. Le quai en bois invite à profiter de l'eau sans fouler l'herbe poussant sur les berges.

Este amplio valle planteaba el reto de proyectar unos baños públicos que afectaran lo menos el entorno natural del río. El muelle de madera invita a disfrutar del agua sin pisar la hierba que crece en la ribera.

Questa ampia vallata presentava la sfida di progettare dei bagni pubblici che incidessero il meno possibile sull'habitat naturale del fiume. Il molo in legno invita a godersi l'acqua senza calpestare l'erba che cresce sulla riva.

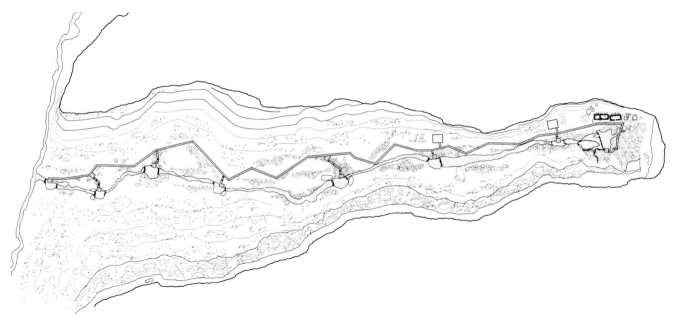

General Plan

Turenscape

Shenyang Architectural University Campus

Location: Shenyang, China   **Completion Year:** 2003   **Photos:** © Kongjian Yu, Chao Yang

The design for the new campus of the University of Shenyang had to respect three fundamental premises: a quick start-to-finish timeframe, a low construction budget, and the architects' desire to evoke the agricultural past of this area, which was once occupied by rice paddies.

Bei der Gestaltung des neuen Campus der Universität Shenyang mussten drei Grundvoraussetzungen beachtet werden: Die Zeit für die Ausführung war sehr kurz, es waren nur wenig finanzielle Mittel vorhanden und die Architekten wollten an die ländliche Vergangenheit des Ortes erinnern, an dem Reis angepflanzt wurde.

Le design du nouveau campus de l'université de Shenyang devait respecter trois prémisses fondamentales : un délai de réalisation court, un budget d'exécution faible et le désir des architectes d'évoquer le passé agricole de l'endroit, dédié autrefois à la riziculture.

El diseño del nuevo campus de de la universidad de Shenyang tenía que respetar tres premisas fundamentales: un corto plazo de realización, un bajo presupuesto de ejecución y el deseo de los arquitectos de evocar el pasado agrícola de esta zona, que se dedicaba a la simbra de arroz.

Il progetto del nuovo campus universitario di Shenyang doveva rispettare tre premesse fondamentali: un breve termine di realizzazione, un ridotto budget operativo e il desiderio degli architetti di evocare il passato agricolo di questa zona, anticamente dedita alla coltivazione del riso.

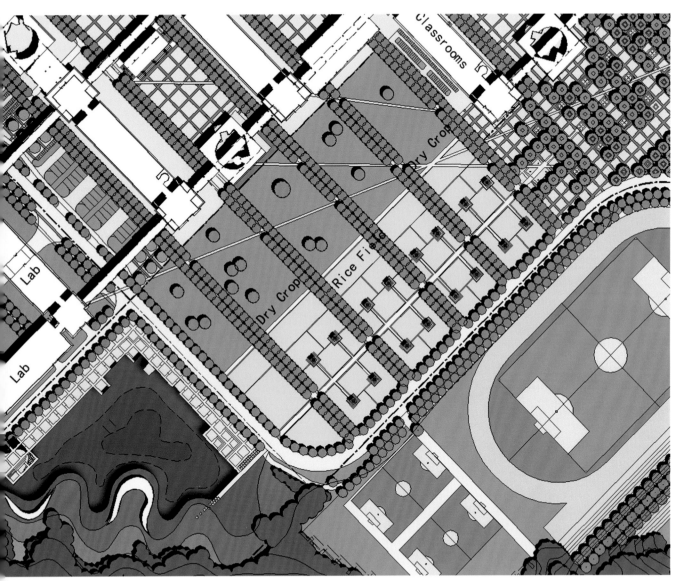

Classrooms

Dry Crop

Dry Crop

Lab

Rice Fi

Lab

General Plan

mcgregor & partners

Former BP Site Waverton

Location: Sydney, Australia Completion Year: 2005 Photos: © Brett Boardman

The old BP oil company site, abandoned for many years, has recently been recovered by creating this recreational and environmental park. The large concrete platforms that were used for the tanks are now plazas that evoke the recent past of the place.

Auf dem ehemaligen Gelände der Ölgesellschaft BP, das viele Jahre lang ungenutzt war, wurde vor kurzem dieser Freizeit- und Umweltpark geschaffen. Die großen Betonplattformen, die für die Tanks benutzt wurden, sind heute Plätze, die an die Vergangenheit des Ortes erinnern.

L'ancien emplacement de la compagnie pétrolière BP, à l'abandon durant plusieurs années, vient d'être récupéré pour créer ce parc de loisirs et environnementales. Les grandes plateformes de béton, utilisées pour les réservoirs, sont aujourd'hui des places parlant du passé récent du lieu.

El antiguo emplazamiento de la industria petrolera BP, abandonado durante muchos años, ha sido recientemente recuperado para crear este parque recreativo y medioambiental. Las grandes plataformas de hormigón que se utilizaban para los tanques son ahora plazas que hablan del pasado reciente del lugar.

L'antica ubicazione dell'industria petrolifera BP, abbandonata per molti anni, è stata recuperata di recente per creare questo piacevole parco ricreativo. Le grandi piattaforme di cemento utilizzate per le cisterne sono adesso piazze che parlano del passato non molto lontano del luogo.

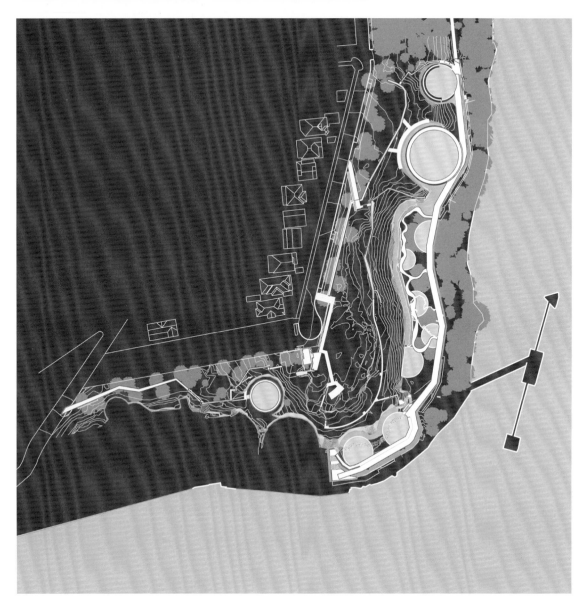

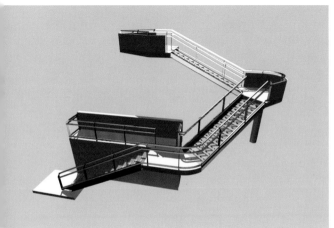

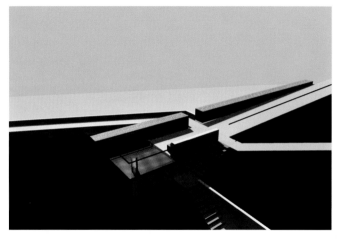

Gustafson Guthrie Nichol

Lurie Garden

Location: Chicago, IL, USA **Completion Year:** 2005 **Photos:** © Gustafson Guthrie Nichol

This garden forms part of Lakefront Millennium Park, an ambitious project for a public space that aimed to combine a number of emblematic pieces in order to create a large area for recreation that would double as a connection between a semi-enclosed facility and the Art Institute of Chicago.

Der Garten gehört zum Lakefront Millennium Park, einem ehrgeizigen Projekt im öffentlichen Raum, in dem verschiedene sinnbildliche Elemente zusammengefügt wurden, um eine große Freizeitanlage zu schaffen. Der Park dient darüber hinaus als Verbindungselement zwischen einer halb abgeschlossenen Zone und dem Art Institute of Chicago.

Le jardin fait partie du parc Lakefront Millennium, un projet ambitieux d'espace public qui assemble diverses pièces emblématiques pour engendrer une grande zone de loisirs et qui fonctionne comme un élément de connexion entre une enceinte semi-couverte et l'Art Institute de Chicago.

El jardín forma parte del parque Lakefront Millennium, un ambicioso proyecto de espacio público que ensambla varias piezas emblemáticas para crear una gran zona de recreo y que funciona como elemento de conexión entre un recinto semicubierto y el Art Institute of Chicago.

Il giardino fa parte del parco Lakefront Millennium, un ambizioso progetto di spazio pubblico che assembla vari pezzi emblematici al fine di creare una grande zona di svago e divertimento che funga da elemento di connessione tra un recinto semicoperto e l'Art Institute of Chicago.

Scapelab

Čufar Square

Location: Jesenice, Slovenia **Completion Year:** 2001 **Photos:** © Miran Kambič

The project that won the competition for the renovation of this plaza was precisely the one whose idea was the farthest away from what was requested: a traditional plaza with a fountain. The bands of color that run across the wavy surface of the pavement still inspire controversy in the city.

Das Projekt, das die Ausschreibung zur Neugestaltung dieses Platzes gewann, war genau jenes, welches sich am weitesten von dem entfernte, was vorgesehen war, ein traditioneller Platz mit einem Brunnen. Die bunten Streifen, die über das gewellte Pflaster verlaufen, sorgen in der Stadt noch immer für Polemiken.

Le projet, lauréat du concours de rénovation de cette place, était précisément celui s'éloignant le plus de ce qui était demandé : une place traditionnelle avec fontaine. Les bandes de couleurs parcourant la superficie ondulée du revêtement demeurent une source de polémique dans la ville.

El proyecto que ganó el concurso para la reforma de esta plaza fue justamente el que más se alejaba de lo que se pedía: una plaza tradicional con fuente. Las bandas de colores que recorren la superficie ondulada del pavimento aún generan polémica en la ciudad.

Il progetto aggiudicatosi la gara di appalto per la ristrutturazione di questa piazza è stato quello che più si allontanava dalla richiesta iniziale: una piazza tradizionale con una fontana. Le strisce colorate che percorrono la superficie ondulata del pavimento sono ancora oggi motivo di polemiche tra gli abitanti della città.

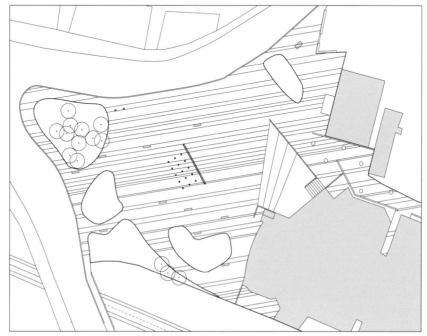

General Plan

Kengo Kuma & Associates

NTT Aoyama Renovation

Location: Tokyo, Japan **Completion Year:** 2004 **Photos:** © Daici Ano

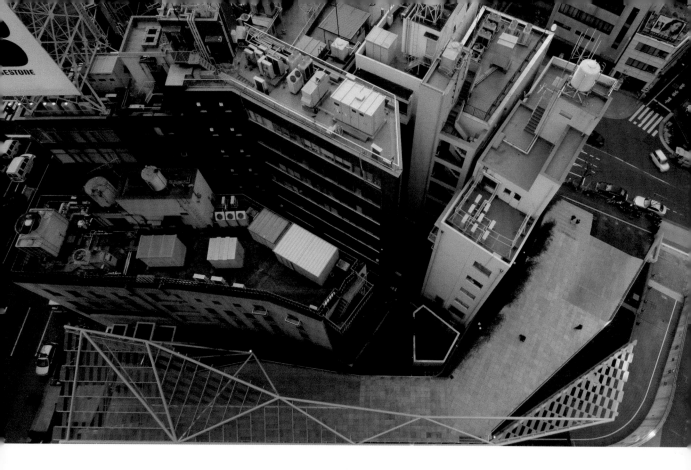

The redevelopment of a pedestrian thoroughfare in the business district of Aoyama entailed the renovation of this public space. To do so, new development—in the form of cafés and small businesses—was planned to encourage visitors to pause when they passed through.

Die Wiederherstellung eines Fußgängerweges im Geschäftsviertel von Aoyama brachte die Renovierung dieses öffentlichen Raumes mit sich. Dazu wurden in der Nachbarschaft neue Cafés und kleine Geschäfte geschaffen, die Besucher zum Verweilen einladen.

La récupération d'un passage piétonnier dans le quartier commercial d'Aoyama impliquait la rénovation de l'espace public. Pour ce, de nouvelles atmosphères ont vu le jour, suscitant les relations sociales, ainsi des cafés ou de petits commerces.

La recuperación de un paseo peatonal en el distrito comercial de Aoyama implicaba la renovación del espacio público. Para ello, se crearon nuevos ámbitos que incentivaran las relaciones sociales como cafés y pequeños comercios.

Il recupero di una strada pedonale nel distretto commerciale di Aoyama comportava il rinnovamento dello spazio pubblico. Per questo, sono stati realizzati nuovi ambiti che incentivassero i rapporti sociali quali caffetterie e piccoli esercizi commerciali.

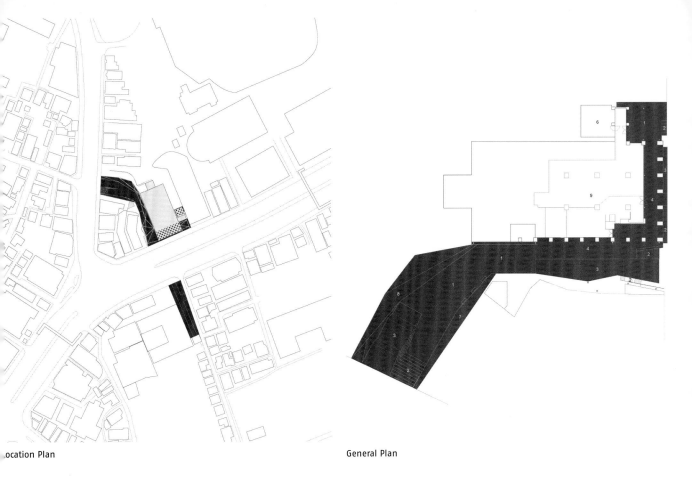

Location Plan

General Plan

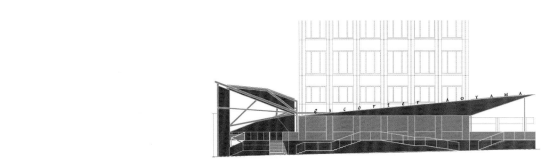

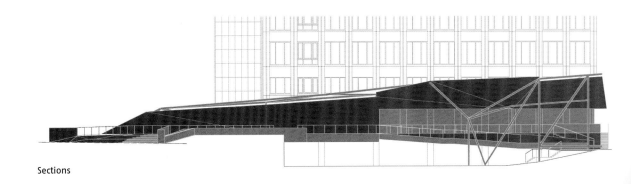

Sections

Rotzler Krebs Partner

Recycling Garden

Location: Winterthur, Switzerland **Completion Year:** 2004 **Photos:** © Rotzler Krebs Partner

The roof of this industrial hangar, which is a collection point for a wide variety of recyclable materials, serves its employees as a parking lot and garden. The lighting and traffic lights are reminiscent of a landing strip.

Das Dach dieser Fabrikhalle, in der verschiedene Recyclingmaterialien gesammelt und verarbeitet werden, dient als Parkplatz und Garten für die Angestellten. Die Beleuchtung und Verkehrssignale erinnern an eine Landebahn.

La couverte de ce hangar industriel dédié à la collecte et à l'élaboration des matériaux les plus divers de recyclage sert de parking et de jardin pour les employés. L'éclairage et la signalisation rappellent une piste d'atterrissage.

La cubierta de este hangar industrial dedicado a la recolección y elaboración de los más diversos materiales de reciclaje es utilizada como aparcamiento y jardín para los empleados. La iluminación y las señales de tráfico recuerdan a una pista de aterrizaje.

La copertura di questo hangar industriale adibito alla raccolta ed elaborazione dei più svariati materiali di riciclaggio viene usata come parcheggio e giardino per i dipendenti. L'illuminazione e la segnaletica ricordano una pista di atterraggio.

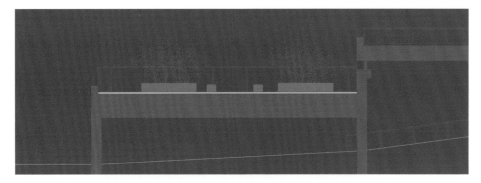

Section

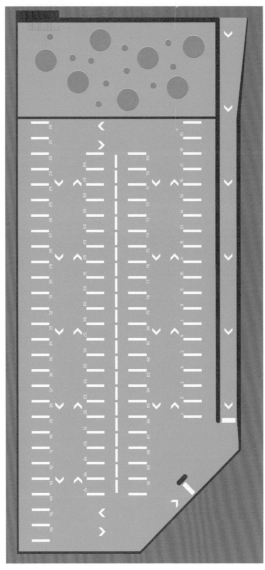

Plan

Levin Monsigny Landschaftsarchitekten

Georg Freundorfer Plaza

Location: Munich, Germany **Completion Year:** 2002

Photos: © Claas Dreppenstedt, Levin Monsigny Landschaftsarchitekten

This project, located in the most densely built part of the city, saw the restoration of an existing park to its original layout, as well as the integration of the buildings that surround the central plaza. The fact that it serves as an urban stage has been emphasized and the plantings have been highlighted.

Diese Anlage befindet sich in dem am dichtesten bebauten Stadtteil. Vorgesehen war die Wiederherstellung eines besteheden Parks in seiner ursprünglichen Anordnung, ebenso sollten die den zentralen Platz umgebenden Gebäudegruppen integriert werden. Der Charakter einer städtischen Bühne wurde unterstrichen und auch die Bepflanzungen wurden betont.

Le projet, situé dans la zone la plus dense de la ville, récupère le caractère du parc originel et intègre l'ensemble d'immeubles l'entourant dans la place centrale. Son caractère de scène urbaine a été renforcé tout en mettant en avant sa végétation.

El proyecto, ubicado en la zona de mayor densidad de la ciudad, recupera el carácter del parque originario e integra el conjunto de edificios que lo rodea en la plaza central. Su carácter de escenario urbano se ha potenciado y se ha puesto en relieve la vegetación.

Il progetto, ubicato nella zona di maggior densità della città, recupera il carattere del parco originario e integra il complesso di edifici circostanti nella piazza centrale. Il suo carattere di scenario urbano è stato potenziato e si è messa in rilievo la vegetazione.

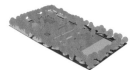

Layers Diagram

General Plan

Renders

Janet Rosenberg & Associates, Carruthers Shaw and Partners

Courthouse Square Park

Location: Toronto, Canada   **Completion Year:** 2000   **Photos:** © Sharon Kish

A project to redevelop an area of the city gave rise to this park, which integrates the surrounding buildings through a series of gardens that are home to different species of plants; each of these gardens establishes a relationship both with its immediate surroundings and the history of the place itself.

Im Zuge der Sanierung eines Viertels der Stadt wurde dieser Park angelegt, der die verschiedenen, umgebenden Gebäude durch eine Reihe von Gärten integriert, die mit verschiedenen Pflanzen angelegt werden. Jeder dieser Gärten stellt eine Beziehung zu seiner unmittelbaren Umgebung und zu der Geschichte des Ortes her.

Le projet de récupération d'une zone de la ville est à l'origine de ce parc qui intègre les diverses édifications l'environnant grâce à une série de jardins où ont été plantées différentes espèces végétales: chacune entame une relation avec son environnement immédiat et l'histoire du lieu.

El proyecto de recuperación de una zona de la ciudad ha dado origen a este parque que integra las diversas edificaciones que lo rodean mediante una serie de jardines donde se plantaron diferentes especies vegetales; cada una de ellas entabla una relación con su entorno inmediato y con la historia del lugar.

Il progetto di recupero di una zona della città ha dato origine a questo parco che integra le diverse costruzioni circostanti mediante una serie di giardini dove sono state piantate diverse specie vegetali; ognuna di loro instaura un rapporto con l'ambiente più immediato e con la storia del posto.

David Chipperfield, B720 Arquitectura

Teruel Urban Development

Location: Teruel, Spain Completion Year: 2003 Photos: © Hisao Suzuki

The objective of this design was to open a section of the city walls of Teruel, Spain to provide a pedestrian throughway to the train station. A very important accomplishment of the project was the incorporation of the elevator and the access elements, which are of a very contemporary style, without disturbing the unity.

Ziel dieses Projektes war es, an einem Teil der Stadtmauer von Teruel eine Öffnung für einen Fußgängerweg zum Bahnhof zu schaffen. Eine sehr wichtige Leistung dabei war, wie perfekt die Planer den Aufzug und die Elemente des Zugangs, die sehr zeitgenössisch sind, in die historische Mauer integrierten, so dass deren Einheitlichkeit nicht unterbrochen wurde.

Le projet avait pour objectif d'intervenir sur une partie des murailles de Teruel afin d'offrir un accès piétonnier à la gare. La réussite principale fut d'incorporer l'ascenseur et les éléments d'accès, à l'esthétique très contemporaine, à un ensemble historique sans rompre son unité.

El objetivo del proyecto era intervenir en un tramo de las murallas de Teruel para proporcionar un acceso peatonal a la estación de trenes. El gran logro fue incorporar el ascensor y los elementos de acceso, de estética marcadamente contemporánea, al conjunto histórico sin romper su unidad.

L'obiettivo del progetto era intervenire su un tratto delle mura di Teruel al fine di ricavare un accesso pedonale alla stazione ferroviaria. Il merito più grande è stato quello di inserire l'ascensore e gli elementi di accesso, di estetica prettamente contemporanea, nel complesso storico senza romperne l'unità.

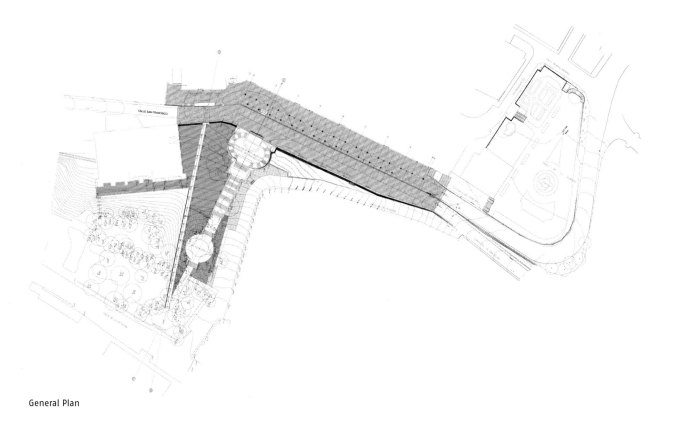

General Plan

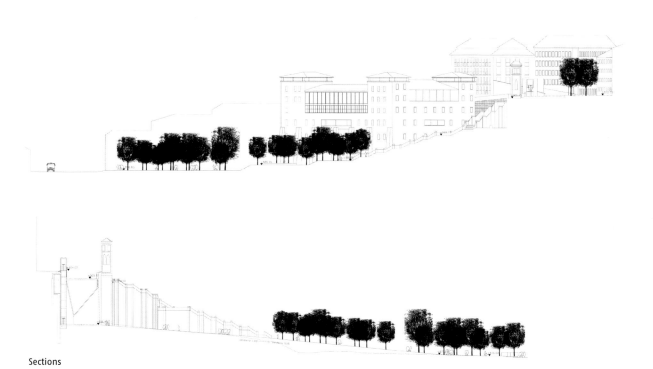

Sections

Dal Pian Arquitectos Associados

Praça das Águas

Location: Campinas, Brazil **Completion Year:** 2004 **Photos:** © Dal Pian Arquitectos Associados

The water company of Campinas organized a competition for the creation of a park to commemorate the installation of the first reservoir of potable water in the city. This design, which makes repeated references to water, proposes several public areas of diverse use.

Das Wasserwerk von Campinas schrieb einen Wettbewerb für einen Gedenkpark aus, der an den Standort der ersten Trinkwasserreserve der Stadt erinnern sollte. In der Gestaltung wird ständig auf das Wasser angespielt und so entstanden öffentliche Bereiche für verschiedene Nutzungsformen.

Les entreprises de l'eau de Campinas ont convoqué un concours pour la réalisation d'un parc commémoratif sur l'emplacement de la première réserve d'eau potable de la ville. Le projet, grâce à des références continues à l'eau, propose des aires publiques aux usages divers.

La empresa de aguas de Campinas convocó un concurso para la realización de un parque conmemorativo en el emplazamiento de la primera reserva de agua potable de la ciudad. El proyecto, que hace continuas referencias al agua, propone unas áreas públicas de diverso uso.

L'azienda che gestisce la rete idrica di Campinas convocò un concorso per la realizzazione di un parco commemorativo nel luogo dove era ubicata la prima riserva di acqua potabile della città. Il progetto, che fa continui riferimenti all'acqua, propone degli spazi pubblici adibiti ad usi diversi.

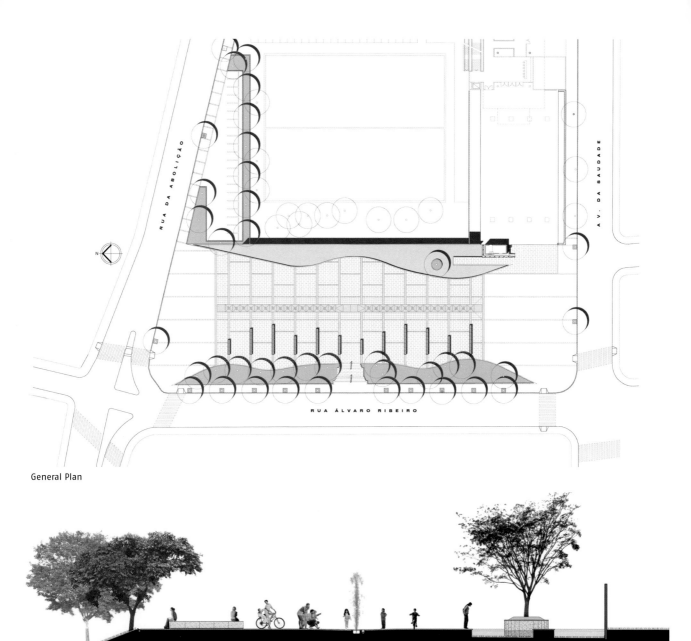

General Plan

ection

evation

Sasaki Associates

Doosan 100 Year Park

Location: Seoul, South Korea **Completion Year:** 2000 **Photos:** © Seung Hoon Yum

This commemorative piece was created in a small plaza in Seoul's historic downtown to celebrate the past, the present, and the future of Doosan, the oldest company in Korea. A curved granite wall, where the names of the subsidiary companies have been engraved, frames the cylinder that stands in the middle of the plaza.

Auf einem kleinen Platz im historischen Zentrum von Seul schuf man dieses Denkmal, das an die Vergangenheit, die Gegenwart und die Zukunft von Doosan erinnert, dem ältesten Unternehmen von Korea. Eine gebogene Granitmauer, in die die Namen der Tochtergesellschaften eingehauen sind, umgibt den Zylinder, der sich mitten auf dem Platz erhebt.

Cette pièce commémorative a été créée dans une petite place du centre historique de Séoul, afin de célébrer le passé, le présent et le futur de Doosan, la plus ancienne compagnie de Corée. Un mur courbe en béton, dans lequel ont été gravés les noms des filiales, encadre le cylindre s'élevant au centre de la place.

En una pequeña plaza del centro histórico de Seúl se creó esta pieza conmemorativa para celebrar el pasado, el presente y el futuro de Doosan, la compañía más antigua de Corea. Una muro curvo de granito, en la que se han grabado los nombres de las compañías subsidiarias, enmarca el cilindro que se alza en medio de la plaza.

In una piccola piazza del centro storico di Seul è stata realizzata questa opera commemorativa per celebrare il passato, il presente e il futuro della Doosan, la più antica compagnia coreana. Un muro curvo in granito, dove sono stati incisi i nomi delle società affiliate, incornicia il cilindro che si erge in mezzo alla piazza.

NO.MAD Arquitectos

Plaza del Desierto

Location: Barakaldo, Spain **Completion Year:** 2002 **Photos:** © Geraldine Bruneel

Here, what was originally an industrial area outside Bilbao was transformed into a residential neighborhood, through the Bilbao Ría 2000 plan. This public space, which is halfway between park and plaza, comprises the central piece of the plan and reuses many of the industrial relics that were found on the site.

Im Rahmen des Planes Bilbao Ría 2000 wurde ein ehemaliges Industriegebiet am Stadtrand von Bilbao in ein Wohnviertel umgestaltet. Im Zentrum des neuen Viertels liegt eine Anlage, die halb Park, halb Platz ist, und in der viele der originalen, industriellen Elemente des Ortes wieder verwendet wurden.

Une ancienne zone industrielle de la banlieue de Bilbao a été convertie en un quartier résidentiel grâce au plan Bilbao Ría 2000. Cet espace public, à mi-chemin du parc et de la place, constitue la pièce centrale du plan et récupère un nombre d'éléments industriels originels du lieu.

Una antigua zona industrial en las afueras de Bilbao ha sido convertida en un barrio de viviendas gracias al plan Bilbao Ría 2000. Este espacio público, a medio camino entre parque y plaza, constituye la pieza central del plan y recupera muchos elementos industriales originales del lugar.

Una vecchia zona industriale alla periferia di Bilbao è stata trasformata in un quartiere abitativo grazie al progetto di sviluppo Bilbao Ría 2000. Questo spazio pubblico, a metà strada tra un parco e una piazza, costituisce il pezzo centrale del progetto e recupera molti elementi industriali originari del posto.

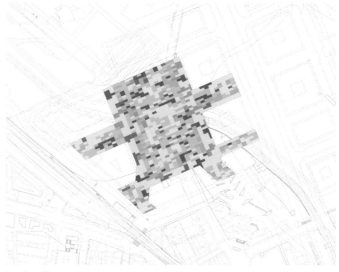

Location Plan

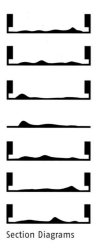

Section Diagrams

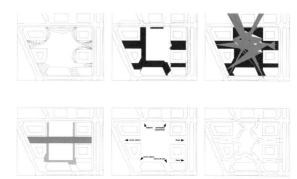

Layers Diagrams

General Plans

NIP paysage

Impluvium

Location: Montreal, Canada **Completion Year:** 2004 **Photos:** © Caroline Issard

This installation, on the roof of a building in downtown Montreal, is a reflection on the potential offered by the tops of city buildings. The last frontier in urban development still waits to be developed by garden designers.

Diese Installation auf der Dachterrasse eines Gebäudes im Zentrum von Montreal stellt eine Art Nachdenken über die Möglichkeiten dar, die die Dächer einer Stadt bieten. Diese letzte Grenze der städtischen Entwicklung wartet noch darauf, durch die Landschaftsgestalter erschlossen zu werden.

Cette installation, sur le toit d'un immeuble du centre de Montréal, se propose comme une réflexion sur le potentiel représenté par les toits des immeubles de la ville : la dernière frontière du développement urbain espère encore être utilisée pour le jardinage.

Esta instalación, en la azotea de un edificio del centro de Montreal, se propone como una reflexión sobre el potencial que representan las cubiertas de los edificios en la ciudad; la última frontera del desarrollo urbano aún espera ser aprovechada por la jardinería.

Questa installazione, nella terrazza di un edificio del centro di Montreal, si propone come una riflessione sul potenziale posseduto dalle coperture degli edifici della città; l'ultima frontiera dello sviluppo urbano nell'attesa di essere sfruttata dal giardinaggio.

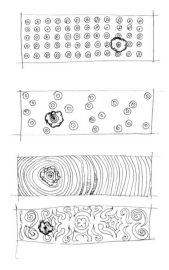

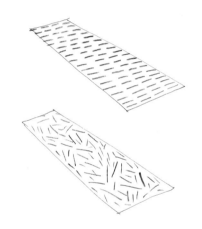

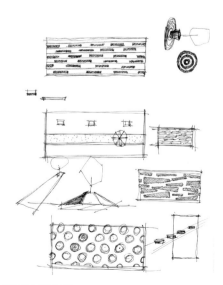

General Diagrams

Plan

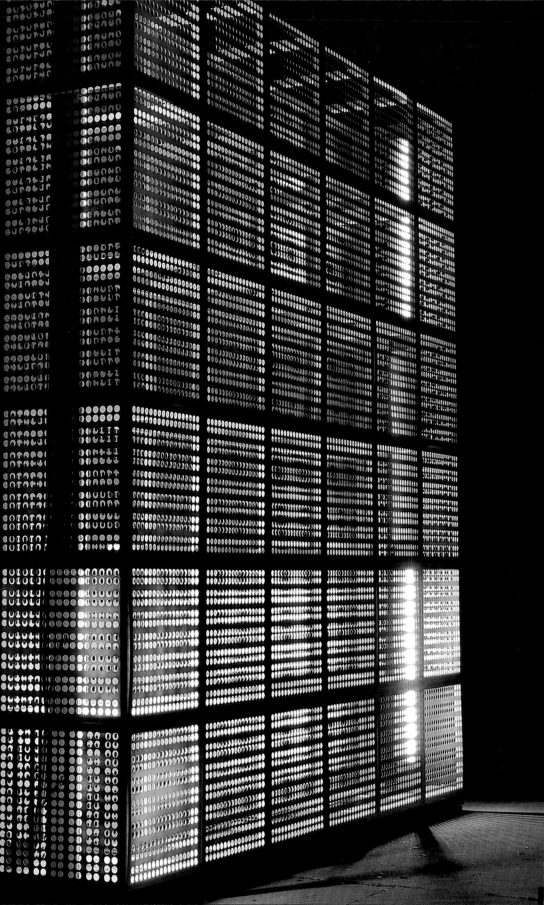

Peter Walker and Partners

Triangle Park

Location: St. Louis, MO, USA **Completion Year:** 2002 **Photos:** © Peter Walker & Partners

An interplay of water, lights, and color serves at the antechamber to the Savvis Center, a setting for entertainment and sporting events that had previously lacked a suitable outdoor space. At night, ten hollow stainless steel panels—which are well-lit and run the length of the semicircular edge of the plaza—generate steam to create a unique atmosphere.

Ein Spiel aus Wasser, Licht und Farben bildet das Vorzimmer zum Savvis Center, eine Freizeit- und Sporteinrichtung, deren Außenanlagen früher nicht attraktiv gestaltet war. Nachts stoßen zehn hohle Edelstahlplatten, die im Halbkreis um den Platz stehen und beleuchtet sind, Dampf aus und schaffen eine suggestive Atmosphäre.

Un jeu d'eau, de lumières et de couleurs sert d'antichambre au Savvis Center, une structure pour événements ludiques et sportifs qui manquait d'un espace extérieur approprié. Durant la nuit, dix panneaux vides en acier inoxydable, disposés tout au long du bord semi-circulaire de la place et opportunément éclairés, diffusent de la vapeur et engendrent une atmosphère évocatrice.

Un juego de agua, luces y colores hace de antesala al Savvis Center, una estructura para acontecimientos lúdicos y deportivos que carecía de un espacio exterior adecuado. Durante la noche, diez paneles huecos de acero inoxidable, dispuestos a lo largo del borde semicircular de la plaza y convenientemente iluminados, despiden vapor y crean una atmósfera sugestiva.

Giochi di luce, acqua e colori fungono da anticamera al Savvis Center, una struttura per eventi ludici e sportivi finora priva di un adeguato spazio esterno. Di sera, dieci pannelli vuoti in acciaio inossidabile, disposti lungo il bordo semicircolare della piazza e adeguatamente illuminati, emettono vapore creando un'atmosfera suggestiva.

Levin Monsigny Landschaftsarchitekten

Market Square

Location: Freyburg, Saxon-Anhalt, Germany **Completion Year:** 2003
Photos: Claas Dreppenstedt, Levin Monsigny Landschaftsarchitekten

This plaza, which is home to an emblematic market, was designated the most important public space in the medieval heart of the city. The surrounding streets were also included in the scope of the project so as to produce an ample, open space that would be paved entirely in limestone.

Dieser Platz, auf dem ein typischer Wochenmarkt stattfindet, sollte zum wichtigsten öffentlichen Raum im mittelalterlichen Zentrum der Stadt werden. Die umgebenden Straßen wurden in die Planung miteinbezogen, um einen offenen und weiten Platz zu schaffen, der ganz mit Kalkstein gepflastert ist.

Cette place, accueillant un marché emblématique, se propose comme l'espace public le plus important du cœur médiéval de la cité. Les rues avoisinantes ont été englobées dans le projet pour obtenir un espace ouvert et vaste, intégralement pavé de pierre calcaire.

Esta plaza, que acoge un emblemático mercado, se propone como el espacio público más importante del corazón medieval de la ciudad. Las calles circundantes se englobaron en el proyecto para obtener un espacio abierto y muy amplio, que se pavimentó enteramente con piedra caliza.

Questa piazza, che ospita un emblematico mercato, si propone come lo spazio pubblico più importante del cuore medievale della città. Le strade circostanti sono state inglobate nel progetto al fine di ottenere uno spazio aperto e molto ampio, che è stato pavimentato interamente con pietra calcarea.

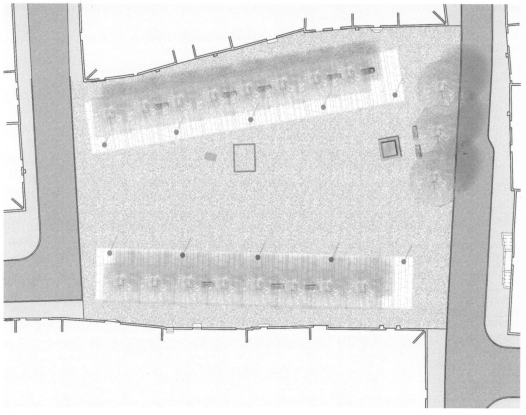

Plan

Rotzler Krebs Partner

Roundabout Obertorplatz

Location: Schaffhausen, Switzerland   **Completion Year:** 2001   **Photos:** © Rotzler Krebs Partner

This traffic circle is situated directly in front of the gates to the historic part of the city, and with a simple composition transforms the intense traffic that passes through it into something scenic. A series of concentric rings, lifted slightly above ground level, reflects the dynamic nature of this spot.

Genau vor einem der Tore zur historischen Altstadt befindet sich dieser Kreisverkehr, auf dem in Form einer einfachen Komposition der intensive Verkehr, der hier herrscht, in Szene gesetzt wird. Einige konzentrische Ringe, die leicht vom Boden abgehoben sind, reflektieren die Dynamik des Ortes.

Juste devant les portes permettant d'accéder au centre historique de la ville, se trouve cette rotonde scénifiant, grâce à une simple composition, l'intense circulation la parcourant. Des anneaux concentriques et légèrement soulevés du sol reflètent le dynamisme de l'endroit.

Justo delante de las puertas a través de las cuales se accede al casco histórico de la ciudad, se encuentra esta rotonda que escenifica, mediante una simple composición, el intenso tráfico que la recorre. Unos anillos concéntricos y ligeramente levantados del suelo reflejan el dinamismo de este lugar.

Proprio davanti alle porte di accesso al centro storico della città, si trova questa rotonda che rappresenta, mediante una semplice composizione, l'intenso traffico che la percorre. Degli anelli concentrici e leggermente alzati da terra rispecchiano il dinamismo di questo luogo.

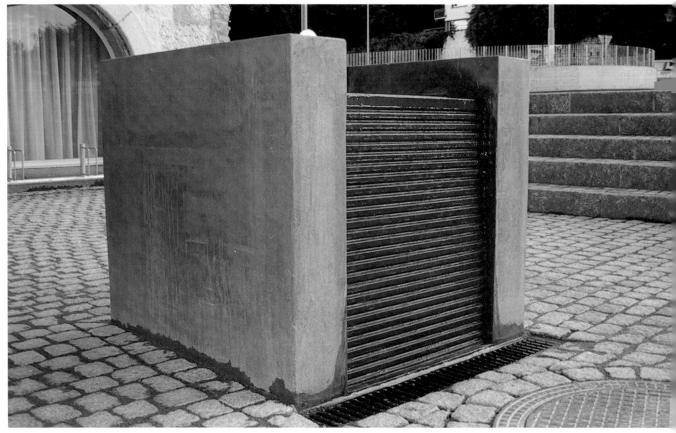

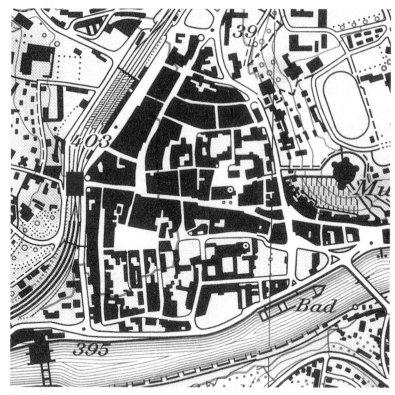

Location Plan

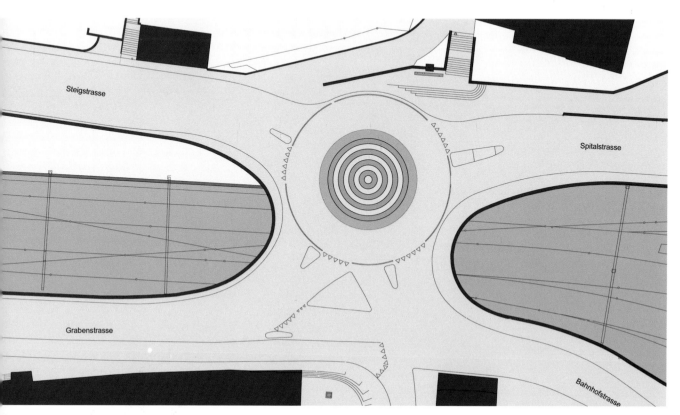

an

Peter Walker and Partners

Saitama Plaza

Location: Tokyo, Japan   **Completion Year:** 2000   **Photos:** © Peter Walker & Partners

This plaza unfolds in the center of a renovated neighborhood in the city, which houses the train station, a stadium and multi-use skyscrapers. Flat surfaces are the characteristic trait of this space, and contrast with the verticality of the surrounding buildings.

Dieser Platz liegt im Zentrum eines restaurierten Viertels der Stadt, in dem sich der Bahnhof, das Stadium und vielseitig genutzte Wolkenkratzer befinden. Ebene Oberflächen, die einen Kontrast zu der Vertikalen der umgebenden Gebäude bilden, kennzeichnen diesen Platz.

Cette place s'ouvre au centre d'une partie rénovée de la ville, accueillant une gare, un stade et des gratte-ciel aux divers usages. Les superficies planes sont le trait caractéristique de cet espace et contrastent avec la verticalité des édifices environnants.

Esta plaza se abre en el centro de una renovada zona de la ciudad, que acoge una estación de trenes, un estadio y rascacielos de uso múltiple. Las superficies planas son el rasgo característico de este espacio y contrastan con la verticalidad de los edificios circundantes.

Questa piazza si apre al centro di una rinnovata zona della città, che ospita una stazione ferroviaria, uno stadio e grattacieli adibiti a vari usi. Le superfici piane sono il tratto caratteristico di questo spazio e contrastano con la verticalità degli edifici circostanti.

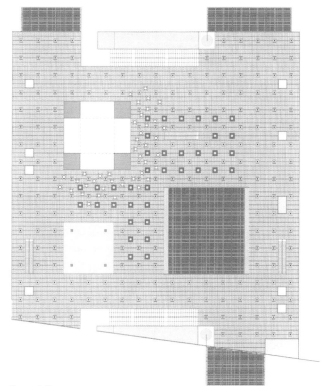

General Plan

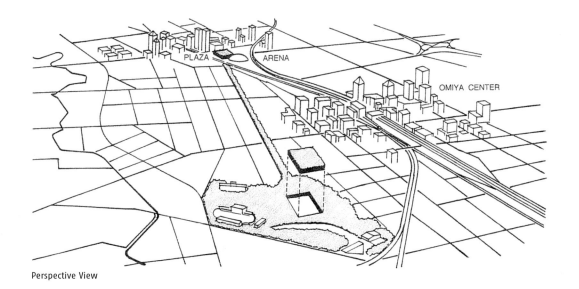

Perspective View

Nande Korpnik

Square in Celjski

Location: Celjski, Slovenia **Completion Year:** 2002 **Photos:** © Damir Fabijanic

This project was based on the idea of restoring the original character of this triangular plaza as a prominent gathering place in the city. The design combines old elements, such as the Roman ruins that are displayed under the glass cupolas, with a contemporary and futuristic language.

Die Idee der Planer war es, dass dieser dreieckige Platz seine Originalstruktur wieder erlangen und zu einem wichtigen Treffpunkt innerhalb der Stadt werden sollte. Bei der Gestaltung wurden antike Elemente wie die römischen Überreste, die unter Glaskuppeln ausgestellt werden, mit einem zeitgenössischen und futuristischen Stil gemischt.

Le projet surgit de l'idée de récupérer le caractère originel de cette place triangulaire comme lieu de rencontre privilégié de la ville. Le design mêle les éléments anciens – ainsi les vestiges romains exposés sous les coupoles de verre – et le langage contemporain et futuriste.

El proyecto surge de la idea de recuperar el carácter original de esta plaza triangular como destacado lugar de encuentro en la ciudad. El diseño mezcla elementos antiguos, como los restos romanos que se exhiben bajo las cúpulas de cristal, con un lenguaje contemporáneo y futurista.

Il progetto nasce dall'idea di recuperare il carattere originale di questa piazza triangolare come importante luogo di ritrovo della città. Il disegno mescola elementi antichi, come i resti romani in mostra sotto la cupola di cristallo, con un linguaggio contemporaneo e futurista.

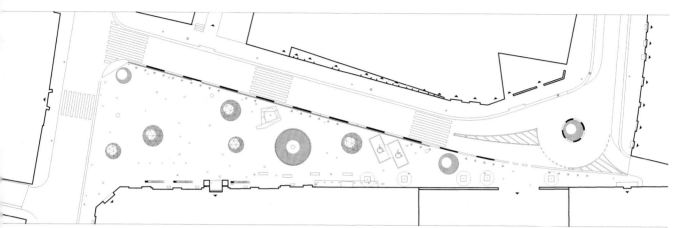

General Plan

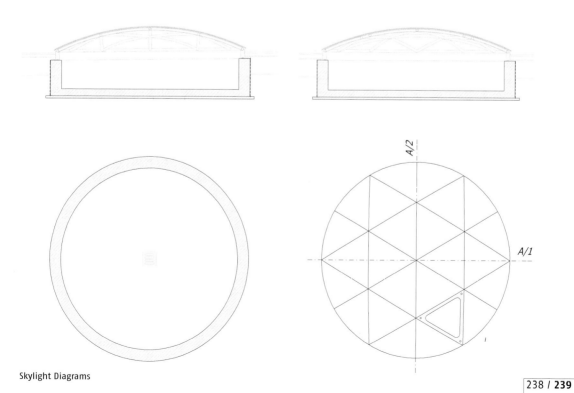

A/2

A/1

Skylight Diagrams

Atelier 4D

Centre of Namur

Location: Namur, Belgium **Completion Year:** 2000 **Photos:** © Jean-Luc Laloux, Atelier 4D

The Place d'Armes fits into the urban layout of this city, which is structured around a central axis. This design aimed for an extremely sober air that would emphasize the peculiar configuration of this public space, and would invite passers-by to walk through it.

Der Place d'Armes fügt sich in die die Gliederung der Stadt ein, die sich um eine zentrale Achse herum erstreckt. Der Platz ist sehr einfach gehalten und die besondere Gestalt dieses öffentlichen Ortes wird so unterstrichen, dass Passanten sich eingeladen fühlen, ihn zu durchqueren.

La Place d'Armes s'intègre à la distribution urbanistique de la ville, structurée autour d'un axe central. Le design parie sur une sobriété extrême qui met en valeur la configuration particulière de l'espace public et invite à s'y promener.

La Place d'Armes encaja en la disposición urbanística de la ciudad, que se estructura alrededor de un eje central. El diseño apuesta por una extrema sobriedad que enfatiza la configuración peculiar del espacio público e invita a recorrerlo.

La Place d'Armes si inserisce alla perfezione nell'assetto urbanistico della città, che si struttura attorno ad un asse centrale. La decorazione punta su un'estrema sobrietà che accentua la peculiare configurazione dello spazio pubblico e invita a percorrerlo.

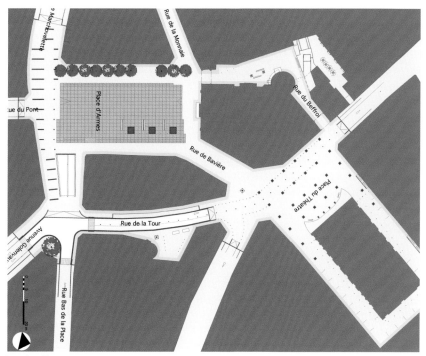

Location Plan

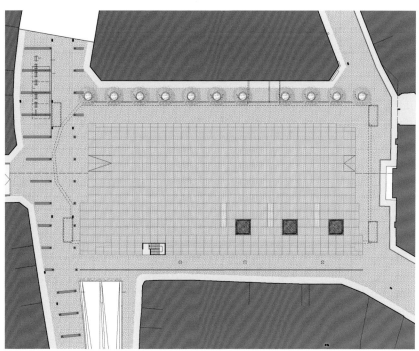

Plan

Shores · Ufer · Rives · Orillas · Sponde

Pere Joan Ravetllat & Carme Ribas Arquitectos

Passeig García Faria

Location: Barcelona, Spain **Completion Year:** 2004 **Photos:** © Roger Casas

This long plaza was designed on a large surface that conceals a highway and a large parking lot right next to the ocean. Faced with the impossibility of incorporating a garden, the project opted for a colorful pavement where the different walking areas are represented.

Auf einer breiten Überdachung, die eine Autobahn und einen großen Parkplatz direkt am Meer verbirgt, wurde dieser längs verlaufende Platz angelegt. Da es nicht möglich war, einen Garten zu schaffen, wurde der Platz bunt gepflastert und so verschiedene Bereiche für den Spaziergang geschaffen.

Cette place longitudinale a été projetée sur une vaste couverte occultant une autoroute et un grand parking, juste à côté de la mer. Face à l'impossibilité de l'aménager en jardin, le projet parie sur un revêtement coloré où se détachent les différentes zones de la promenade.

Sobre una amplia cubierta que oculta una autopista y un gran aparcamiento, justo al lado del mar, se ha proyectado esta plaza longitudinal. Ante la imposibilidad de ajardinarla, el proyecto apuesta por un pavimento colorista donde destacan las diferentes zonas del paseo.

Su un'ampia copertura dietro cui si nascondono un'autostrada e un grande parcheggio, proprio accanto al mare, è stata progettata questa piazza longitudinale. Vista l'impossibilità di realizzarvi dei giardini, il progetto punta su una pavimentazione coloristica che mette in risalto le diverse zone della passeggiata.

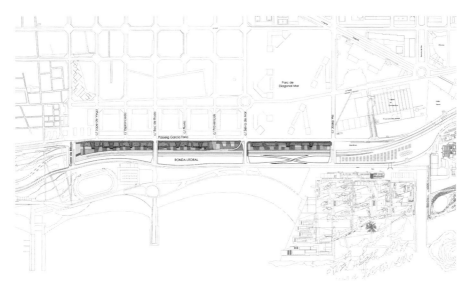

Location Plan

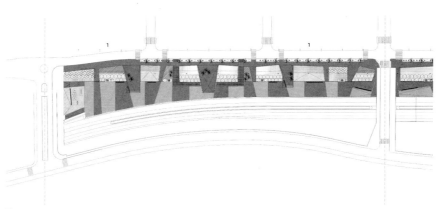

Plan

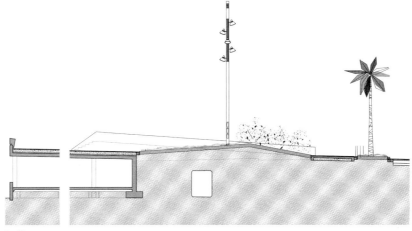

Section

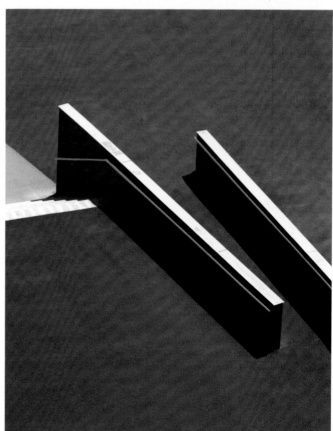

David Irwin/Isthmus Group, Chris Kelly/Architecture Workshop

Oriental Bay Enhancement

Location: Wellington, New Zealand **Completion Year:** 2003 **Photos:** © Nik Kneale, Simon Devitt

These reinforced concrete platforms, located at a strategic point in the bay, serve two functions: they create an artificial reef—which was necessary to create new beaches—and they also serve as an urban landmark and as a setting for recreational activities.

Die Plattformen aus Stahlbeton, die sich an strategischen Punkten in der Bucht befinden, erfüllen zwei Funktionen. Zum einen schaffen sie ein künstliches Riff, das für die Entstehung neuer Strände notwendig ist, andererseits prägen sie das Stadtbild und dienen als Ort der Entspannung.

Les plateformes de béton armé disposées en un point stratégique de la baie remplissent deux fonctions : d'une part créer un récif artificiel nécessaire à la création de nouvelles plages et, d'autre part, servir de référence urbaine et de site de loisirs.

Las plataformas de hormigón armado colocadas en un punto estratégico de la bahía cumplen dos funciones: por una parte, crean un arrecife artificial necesario para la creación de nuevas playas, por otra, sirven de referente urbano y se utilizan como lugar de recreo.

Le piattaforme in cemento armato collocate in un punto strategico della baia svolgono due funzioni: da una parte, formano una scogliera artificiale necessaria per la creazione di nuove spiagge e, dall'altra, servono da referente urbano e come luogo di svago e divertimento.

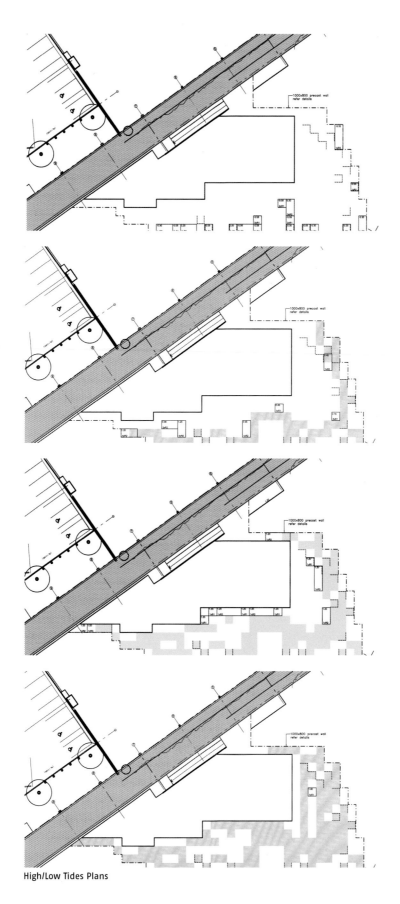

High/Low Tides Plans

Foreign Office Architects

Yokohama International Port Terminal

Location: Yokohama, Japan **Completion Year:** 2002 **Photos:** © Nácasa & Partners

This design suggests mediation between garden and bay through the union of two social environments: the system of the city's public spaces and the continuous flow of passengers through the port. It is the first and most important penetration of the city's public space into the bay.

Das Projekt schlägt eine Vermittlung zwischen Garten und Bucht vor, indem beide soziale Umgebungen verbunden werden, das System der öffentlichen Räume der Stadt und der ständige Verkehr der Passagiere im Hafen. Es handelt sich um das erste und wichtigste Eindringen öffentlichen Raums der Stadt in die Bucht.

Le projet suggère une médiation entre jardin et baie en établissant un lien entre les deux environnements sociaux : le système des espaces publics de la ville et le flux continu de passagers du port. C'est la première et la plus importante compénétration de l'espace public de la ville et de la baie.

El proyecto sugiere una mediación entre jardín y bahía mediante una vinculación de dos entornos sociales: el sistema de espacios públicos de la ciudad y el continuo flujo de pasajeros del puerto. Es la primera y más importante penetración del espacio público de la ciudad en la bahía.

Il progetto suggerisce un collegamento tra il giardino e la baia mediante il vincolo tra due ambienti sociali: il sistema di spazi pubblici della città e il continuo flusso dei passeggeri del porto. È la prima e più importante penetrazione da parte dello spazio pubblico della città nella baia.

Location Plan

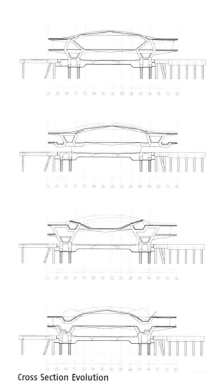

Cross Section Evolution

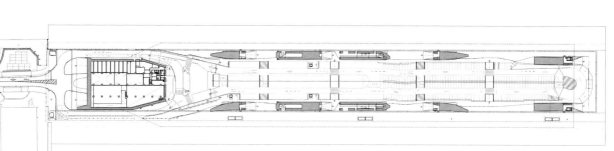

Private Level Plan

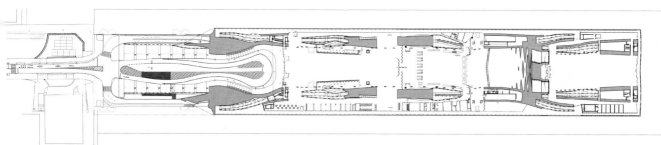

Public Hall Plan

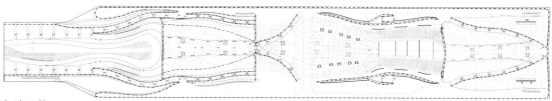

Outdoor Plan

Thorbjörn Andersson, PeGe Hillinge/SWECO FFNS Architects

Dania Park

Location: Malmö, Sweden **Completion Year:** 2002

Photos: © Åke E:son Lindman, Lena Ason, Ulf Celander, Jens Linde

The Malmö waterfront, like many other European ports, had turned its back on the city for many years. This project not only helped rescue a deteriorated area, it also gave the city one of its main public spaces and provided its inhabitants with the opportunity to enjoy the spectacular landscape.

Wie in vielen anderen Häfen Europas war die Küste vor Malmö viele Jahre lang nicht ins Stadtbild integriert. Dieses Projekt diente nicht nur zur Sanierung der verlassenen Gegend, sondern die Stadt bekam auch ein neues, sehr wichtiges öffentliches Gebiet, in dem die Bevölkerung eine wundervolle Landschaft genießen kann.

La façade maritime de Malmö, comme celle de nombreux ports européens, a tourné le dos pendant de nombreuses années à la ville. Ce projet a permis non seulement de récupérer une zone détériorée mais aussi d'offrir à la ville un de ses principaux espaces publics et à la population la chance de profiter d'un paysage spectaculaire.

El frente marítimo de Malmö, igual que el de muchos puertos europeos, dio la espalda a la ciudad durante muchos años. Con este proyecto no sólo se recuperó un área deteriorada, sino que se proporcionó a la ciudad uno de sus principales espacios públicos y a la población la oportunidad de disfrutar del espectacular paisaje.

Il fronte marittimo di Malmö, al pari di quello di molti altri porti europei, aveva dato per tanti anni le spalle alla città. Grazie a questo progetto non solo si è recuperata un'area degradata ma si è restituito alla città uno dei suoi principali spazi pubblici dando inoltre la possibilità agli abitanti di godere dello straordinario paesaggio.

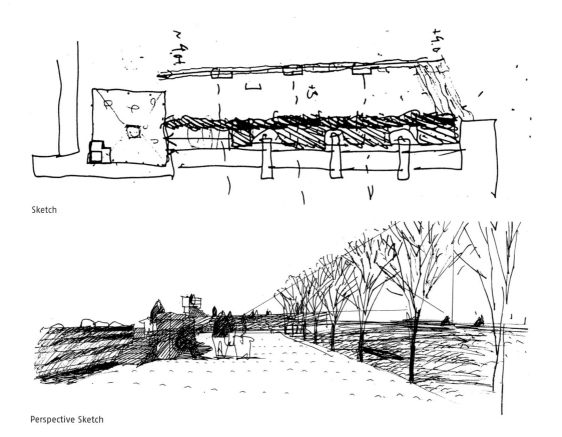

Sketch

Perspective Sketch

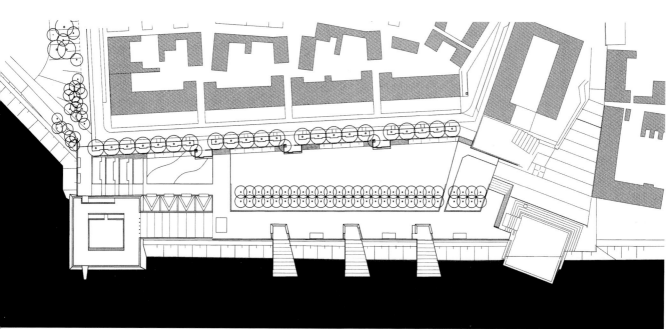

General Plan

Birk Nielsens Tegnestue

Århus City Centre

Location: Århus, Denmark Completion Year: 2003 Photos: © Birk Nielsens Tegnestue

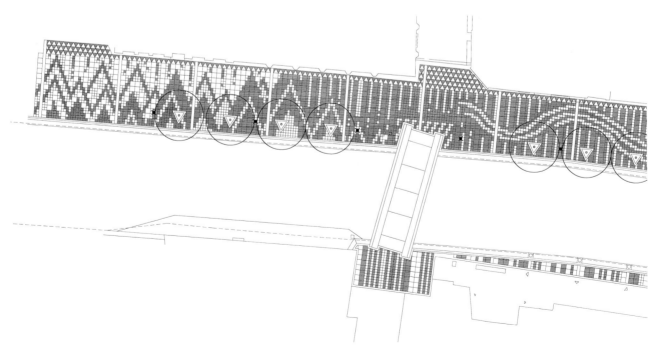

This project proposed the reopening of the old riverbed, which was covered in the 1930s to create a road for quick access to the downtown area. The retaining walls were treated as a compositional element and used to create platforms, fountains, and stairways.

Ziel dieses Projektes war es, einen ehemaligen Flusslauf, der in der Zeit um 1930 bedeckt wurde, um eine Schnellstraße als Zufahrt ins Zentrum zu schaffen, wieder herzustellen. Die Stützmauern wurden als Gestaltungselement benutzt um Plattformen, Quellen und Freitreppen anzulegen.

Le projet propose la récupération de l'antique lit d'une rivière, couvert dans les années 1930 pour créer une voie rapide d'accès au centre. Les murs de contention ont été utilisés comme matériau de composition et génèrent des plateformes, fontaines et escaliers.

El proyecto plantea la recuperación del antiguo cauce de un río que en la década de 1930 se cubrió para crear una rápida vía de acceso al centro. Los muros de contención han sido utilizados como material compositivo y generan plataformas, fuentes y escalinatas.

Il progetto prevede il recupero dell'antico letto di un fiume che negli anni 30 era stato coperto per creare una rapida via di accesso al centro. I muri di contenimento, utilizzati come materiale compositivo, danno vita a piattaforme, fontane e scalinate.

Sasaki Associates

Indianapolis Waterfront

Location: Indianapolis, IN, USA **Completion Year:** 2000 **Photos:** © Barnett Photography

This project transformed the banks of the White River, where it flows through the city of Indianapolis, into a series of open spaces that connect the main civic centers of the city with the river. The design incorporates elements that are reminiscent of the place's old use.

Das Ufer des White River in der Stadt Indianapolis wurde in ein System offener Räume umgestaltet, das die wichtigsten Verwaltungszentren der Stadt mit dem Fluss verbindet. Bei der Gestaltung wurden Elemente benutzt, die an die ehemalige Nutzung des Ortes erinnern.

La rivière de White River, à son passage par la ville d'Indianapolis, a été transformée grâce à ce projet en un système d'espaces ouverts reliant les principaux centres civiques de la ville avec la rivière. Le design incorpore des éléments rappelant les anciens usages du lieu.

La ribera del White River, a su paso por la ciudad de Indianápolis, ha sido transformada, gracias a este proyecto, en un sistema de espacios abiertos que enlazan los principales centros cívicos de la ciudad con el río. El diseño incorpora elementos que recuerdan los antiguos usos del lugar.

Le sponde del White River, nel tratto che attraversa la città di Indianapolis, sono state trasformate, grazie a questo progetto, in un sistema di spazi aperti che collegano le principali circoscrizioni amministrative della città con il fiume. Il disegno incorpora elementi che ricordano le antiche usanze del posto.

Taylor Cullity Lethlean

Birrarung Marr

Location: Melbourne, Australia **Completion Year:** 2002 **Photos:** © Ben Wrigley, John Gollings

It will take years before the plantings in a park are fully grown and established. The redesign of this park in Melbourne, which aimed to transform it into an emblematic park for the city, saw autochthonous species—such as eucalyptus trees—accompanied by carefully laid out leisure areas and reflecting pools.

Die Vegetation in einem Park braucht mehrere Jahre, um sich zu entwickeln und Gestalt anzunehmen. Dieser Park in Melbourne sollte zu einem emblematischen Ort für die Stadt werden. Einheimische Pflanzen wie Eukalyptus unterstreichen die ausgewogene Verteilung von Ruhezonen und reflektierenden Wasserflächen.

La végétation qui constitue un parc a besoin de plusieurs années pour se développer et se consolider. Dans ce parc de Melbourne, prétendant se convertir en un lieu emblématique pour la ville, des espèces autochtones comme l'eucalyptus sont accompagnées d'une distribution judicieuse des aires de repos et des miroirs dans l'eau.

La vegetación que constituye un parque tarda varios años en desarrollarse y consolidarse. En este parque de Melbourne, que se pretende convertir en un lugar emblemático para la ciudad, especies autóctonas como el eucalipto se acompañan con una acertada distribución de las zonas de descanso y de los espejos de agua.

Ci vogliono vari anni per far sviluppare e consolidare la vegetazione di un parco. In questo parco di Melbourne, che si intende trasformare in un luogo emblematico per la città, alle specie autoctone come l'eucalipto fa da sfondo l'accurata distribuzione delle zone di riposo e degli specchi d'acqua.

Studio 3LHD

Memorial Bridge

Location: Rijeka, Croatia **Completion Year:** 2001 **Photos:** © 3LHD, Aljosa Brajdic

The fundamental goal of this project was to bestow a functional object with a monumental character; this modest bridge, which is as high as it is long, was converted into an architectural reference point for the entire village.

Das Hauptziel bei dieser Planung war es, ein funktionelles Objekt monumental wirken zu lassen. Diese bescheidene Brücke, die so hoch wie lang ist, wurde zu einem architektonischen Referenzpunkt des Dorfes.

Le projet avait pour objectif fondamental de conférer un caractère monumental à un objet fonctionnel; ce modeste pont, aussi haut que long, a été converti en point de référence architectural pour tout le village.

El objetivo fundamental del proyecto era conferir un carácter monumental a un objeto funcional; este modesto puente, que mide lo mismo en altura que en longitud, ha sido convertido en un punto de referencia arquitectónico para todo el pueblo.

L'obiettivo fondamentale del progetto era conferire un carattere monumentale a un oggetto funzionale; questo modesto ponte, di identica lunghezza ed altezza, è stato trasformato in un punto di riferimento architettonico per tutto il paese.

Taylor Cullity Lethlean

Geelong Waterfront

Location: Geelong, Australia Completion Year: 2001 Photos: © Peter Hyatt

This intervention emphasizes the role had by the bay—which is constantly evolving—on the urban setting that surrounds it, through a wide variety of textures and shapes that accompany flexible and multifunctional spaces, such as the link between the center of the city and the port.

Durch den Eingriff wurde unterstrichen, welche Rolle diese Bucht in der ständigen Entwicklung ihrer städtischen Umgebung spielt. Die flexiblen und multifunktionalen Räume sind mit Materialien von vielfältiger Textur und in verschiedenen Formen gestaltet und verbinden so das Stadtzentrum und den Hafen.

L'intervention souligne le rôle joué par cette baie en perpétuelle évolution dans le cadre urbain qui l'accueille, grâce à une grande diversité de textures et de formes qui accompagne des espaces flexibles et multifonctionnels, ainsi la liaison entre le centre-ville et le port.

La intervención enfatiza el papel que desempeña esta bahía en constante evolución en el entorno urbano en que se ubica, mediante una gran variedad de texturas y formas que acompaña espacios flexibles y multifuncionales, como el enlace entre el centro de la ciudad y el puerto.

L'intervento risalta il ruolo svolto da questa baia, in costante evoluzione nell'ambiente urbano che l'accoglie, mediante una grande varietà di composizioni e forme che accompagna spazi flessibili e multifunzionali, come la connessione tra il centro della città e il porto.

Aerial View

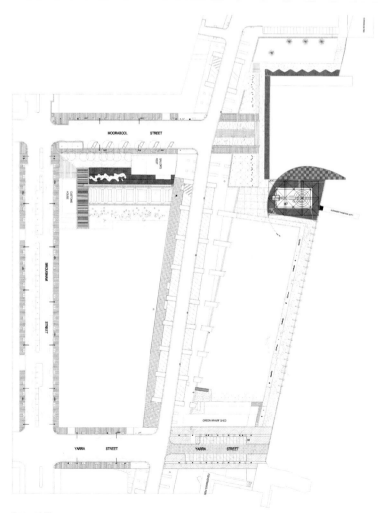

General Plan

Wraight & Associates

Taranaki Wharf

Location: Wellington, New Zealand **Completion Year:** 2005 **Photos:** © Grant Sheehan, Adrian Lamb, Neil Price

The main elements in the design of this project create a connection between the financial district of the city and the bay. A varied repertoire of public spaces—including bridges, waterfront avenues, platforms, and green areas—brings out the best in the surrounding area.

Die wichtigsten Gestaltungselemente bei diesem Projekt dienen der Verbindung zwischen dem Finanzdistrikt der Stadt und der Bucht. Ein vielseitiges Repertoire an öffentlichen Anlagen wie Brücken, Meerespromenaden, Plattformen und Grünzonen bringen das Beste ihrer Umgebung hervor.

Les principaux éléments du design de ce projet servent à créer une connexion entre le quartier financier de la ville et la baie. Une répertoire riche en espaces publics, ainsi des ponts, promenades maritimes, plateformes et espaces verts, tire le meilleur parti de l'environnement les accueillant.

Los principales elementos del diseño de este proyecto sirven para crear una conexión entre el distrito financiero de la ciudad y la bahía. Un variado repertorio de espacios públicos, como puentes, paseos marítimos, plataformas y zonas verdes, sacan el mayor partido del entorno en que se ubican.

I principali elementi di questo progetto servono a creare una connessione tra il distretto finanziario della città e la baia. Uno svariato repertorio di spazi pubblici, come ponti, lungomari, piattaforme e zone verdi, sfrutta al meglio l'ambiente in cui è situato.

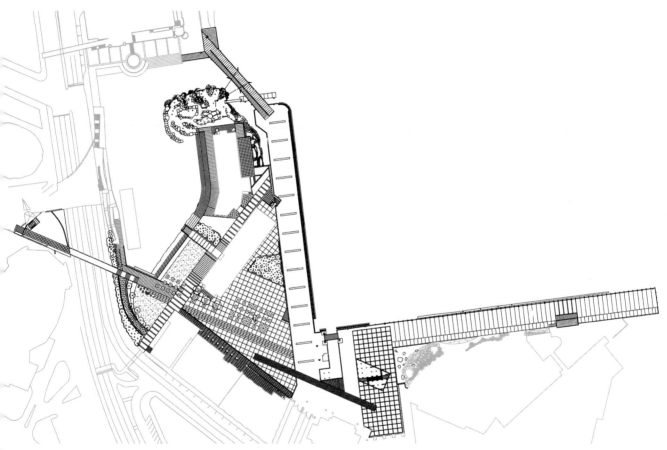

General Plan

Taylor Cullity Lethlean, Tonkin Zuilakha Greer, Robert Owen

Craigieburn Bypass
Urban Design

Location: Melbourne, Australia **Completion Year:** 2005 **Photos:** © John Gollings, Peter Hyatt, Robert Owen

This project is part of a public initiative to create a highway to link the northern part of Melbourne to downtown. The design explores the aesthetic and perceptive possibilities of a wide range of objects—such as bridges, curtain walls, or gardens—when observed from rapid-moving means of transportation.

Durch eine öffentliche Initiative wurde eine Autobahn geschaffen, die den Norden von Melbourne mit der Stadtmitte verbindet. Bei der Gestaltung wurden die ästhetischen Möglichkeiten und Perspektiven verschiedener Objekte wie Brücken, Trennmauern und Gärten erforscht, wenn man sie von einem Fahrzeug, das sich schnell bewegt, aus beobachtet.

Ce projet fait partie d'une initiative publique de création d'autoroute reliant le nord de Melbourne avec le centre-ville. Le design explore les possibilités esthétiques et perceptives de divers objets, ainsi des ponts, pans de murs ou jardins, s'ils sont observés de un moyen de transport se déplaçant à grande vitesse.

Este proyecto es parte de una iniciativa pública para crear una autopista que conecte el norte de Melbourne con el centro de la ciudad. El diseño explora las posibilidades estéticas y perceptivas de diversos objetos, como puentes, muros cortina o jardines, cuando son observados desde un medio de transporte que se desplaza rápidamente.

Questo progetto fa parte di un'iniziativa pubblica volta a creare un'autostrada che colleghi il nord di Melbourne con il centro della città. La sua esecuzione esplora le possibilità estetiche e percettive di diversi oggetti, quali ponti, curtain walls o giardini, quando questi vengono osservati da un mezzo di trasporto che si sposta rapidamente.

Turenscape

Zhongshan Shipyard Park

Location: Zhongshan, China **Completion Year:** 2001 **Photos:** © Kongjian Yu, Chao Yang

Here, along one of China's main rivers, what was originally an industrial area served as the platform for the creation of this enormous park, which created a hitherto inexistent connection point between city and river.

Ein ehemaliges Industriegelände am Ufer einer der wichtigsten Flüsse Chinas diente als Ausgangspunkt für die Anlage dieses Parks mit enormem Ausmaß, der eine Verbindung zwischen der Stadt und dem Fluss schuf, die es bisher noch nicht gab.

Une ancienne zone industrielle sur les rives de l'un des principaux fleuves de Chine a servi de point de départ à la création de ce parc très étendu, créant un point de connexion, jusqu'alors inexistant, entre la ville et le fleuve.

Una antigua zona industrial a orillas de uno de los principales ríos de China ha sido el punto de partida para la creación de este parque de grandes proporciones, que crea un punto de conexión, hasta hace poco inexistente, entre la ciudad y el río.

Un'antica zona industriale sulla riva di uno dei fiumi principali della Cina è stata il punto di partenza per la creazione di questo parco di grandi dimensioni, che genera un punto di connessione, finora inesistente, tra la città e il fiume.

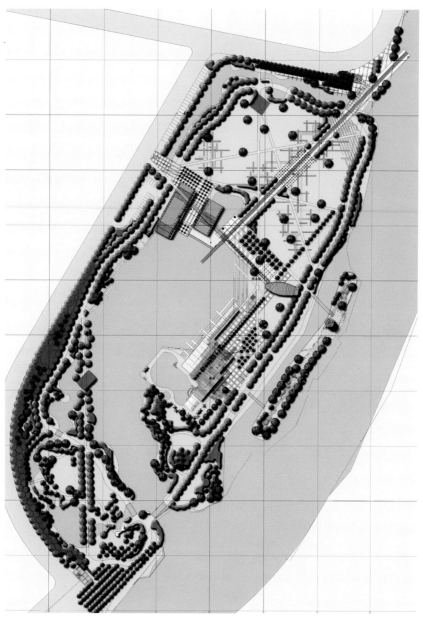

General Plan

StoA Architecture

Remodelling of
Rauba Capeu Pier

Location: Nice, France **Completion Year:** 2003 **Photos:** © Jean-Michel Landecy

The redevelopment of the rockiest part of Nice's waterfront gave the designers the chance to emphasize Rauba Capeu wharf's status as a balcony overlooking the Mediterranean. The project entailed the continuation of the avenue along the waterfront, and the construction of a bike lane and a swimming area, by placing concrete slabs reminiscent of beds amidst the rocks.

Bei der Wiederherstellung der Küste vor Nizza hatte man am steinigsten Abschnitt die Möglichkeit, den guten Ruf, den der Quai Rauba Capeu als Balkon über das Mittelmeer genießt, noch zu steigen. Die Meerespromenade wurde hier fortgesetzt, indem ein Radweg und ein Badebereich geschaffen wurden, in dem sich Betonplatten wie Liegen zwischen den Felsen befinden.

La récupération du front de mer à Nice, sur sa partie la plus rocheuse, a offert la chance de souligner la réputation de balcon sur la Méditerranée dont jouit le quai Rauba Capeu. Le projet a permis de mener à bien la poursuite de la promenade maritime, de construire une piste cyclable et de prévoir une zone de bain avec des planches de béton en forme de lit, entre les rochers.

La recuperación del frente marítimo de Niza, en su tramo más rocoso, ofreció la oportunidad de enfatizar la fama de balcón sobre el Mediterráneo de la que goza el quai Rauba Capeu. Con el proyecto se llevó a cabo la continuación del paseo marítimo, se construyó un carril para las bicicletas y se acondicionó una zona de baño, disponiendo planchas de hormigón a modo de camas entre las rocas.

Il recupero del fronte marittimo di Nizza, nel suo tratto più roccioso, ha offerto la possibilità di incrementare la fama di balcone sul Mediterraneo di cui gode già il quai Rauba Capeu. Con il progetto è stata portata a termine la continuazione del lungomare, è stata costruita una pista ciclabile per le biciclette ed è stata allestita una zona per bagnanti, disponendo delle passerelle di cemento, a guisa di letti, tra le rocce.

Location View

Sections

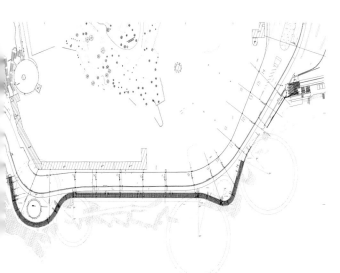

General Plan

Detail Plan

Pierre Lafon

Remodelling of River Bank

Location: Redon, France **Completion Year:** 2004 **Photos:** © Pierre Lafon

In this project, the water's edge was reconfigured to prevent flooding caused when the river over-flowed its banks, in addition to extending the promenade along the river. The narrow stretch of earth available made it necessary for the pedestrian path and bike lane to be superimposed on top of one another.

Das Ufer wurde umgestaltet, um Überschwemmungen beim Übertreten des Flusses zu vermeiden und gleichzeitig den Spazierweg am Fluss entlang zu verlängern. Da nur ein schmaler Streifen Erde zur Verfügung stand, war es notwendig, den Fußgängerweg und den Fahrradweg übereinander zu legen.

La rive fut rénovée pour éviter les inondations produites par les crues de la rivière et, en même temps, prolonger la promenade fluviale. L'étroite frange de terre disponible rendit nécessaire la superposition de la zone piétonnière et de la piste cyclable.

La orilla fue remodelada para prevenir las inundaciones producidas por las crecidas del río y, al mismo tiempo, para prolongar el paseo fluvial. La estrecha franja de tierra disponible hizo que fuera necesario superponer la zona para peatones y el carril de bicicletas.

La sponda è stata ristrutturata al fine di prevenire le inondazioni causate dalle piene del fiume e, al contempo, prolungare il lungofiume. Per via della stretta striscia di terra disponibile è stato necessario sovrapporre la zona pedonale e la pista ciclabile.

Paolo L. Bürgi

Kreuzlingen Hafenplatz

Collaborator: Giorgio Aeberli Location: Kreuzlingen, Switzerland Completion Year: 2003
Photos:© Giosanna Crivelli, Thomas Gut, Paolo L. Bürgi

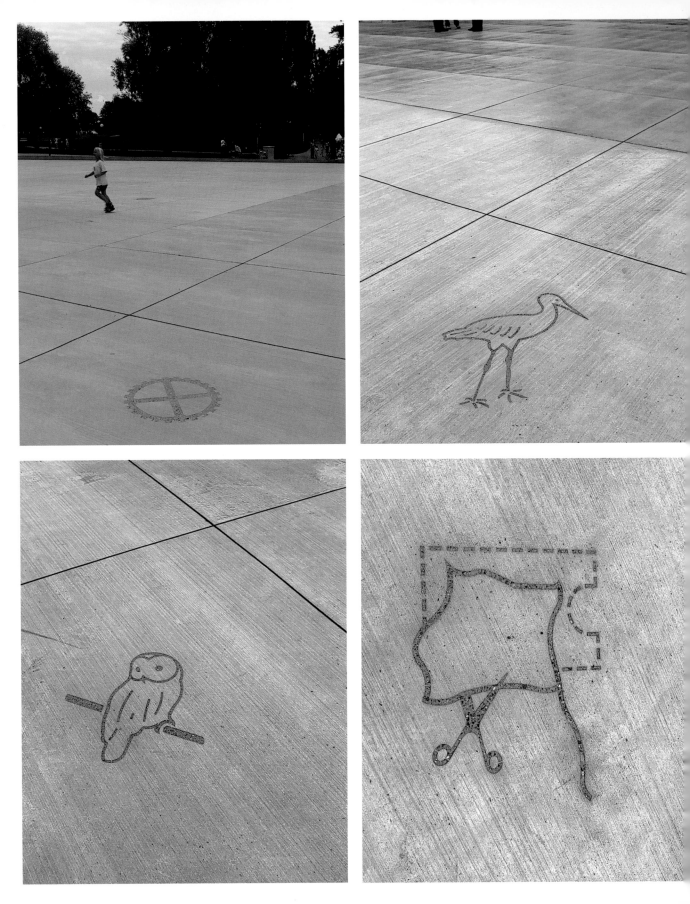

The design of this plaza forges a new relationship between the urban environment and nature; a concrete ramp submerges softly into the water of the lake, and invites passers-by to rest and enjoy the panorama from a series of colorful lounge chairs.

Durch die Gestaltung des Platzes entstand eine neue Beziehung zwischen der städtischen Umgebung und der Natur. Eine Betonrampe geht allmählich im Wasser des Sees unter und lädt die Spaziergänger zum Ausruhen oder zum Genießen der Aussicht in den aufgestellten, bunten Liegestühlen ein.

Le design de la place propose une nouvelle relation entre le cadre urbain et la nature : une rampe de béton se submerge doucement dans les eaux du lac et invite les passants à se reposer et à profiter du panorama depuis l'une des chaises longues de couleur.

El diseño de la plaza propone una nueva relación entre el entorno urbano y la naturaleza; una rampa de hormigón se sumerge suavemente en las aguas del lago e invita a los paseantes a descansar y a disfrutar del panorama desde unas tumbonas de colores.

Il disegno della piazza propone un nuovo rapporto tra l'ambiente urbano e la natura; una rampa in cemento si sommerge leggermente nelle acque del lago e invita i passanti a riposare in delle sdraio colorate da cui godersi il panorama.

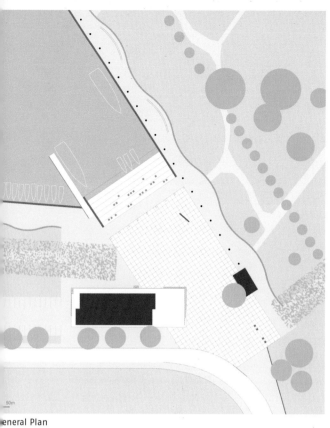

eneral Plan

Bank Detail

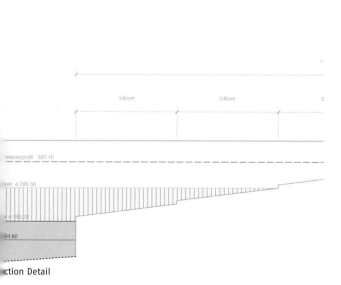

ction Detail

340cm 340cm

wasserprofil 397.10

ner ø 396.50

ø 396.20

94.60

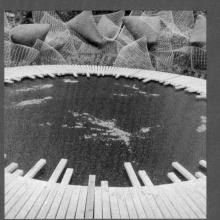

Gardens · Gärten · Jardins · Jardines · Giardini

Architects: Jean-Michel Landecy, Nicolas Deville, Jean-Marc Anzévui
Landscape: Henri Bava, Michel Hoessler, Oliver Philippe

Louis-Jeantet Foundation Garden

Location: Geneve, Switzerland Completion Year: 2000 Photos: © Jean-Michel Landecy

The design for this medical foundation, which was awarded by public competition in 1992, revolves around three basic themes: the renovation of an old neo-Renaissance villa to house the foundation's headquarters, the construction of a new auditorium, and the design of a garden that structures the entire project.

Das Bauprojekt für diese medizinische Stiftung, das 1992 eine öffentliche Ausschreibung gewann, konzentriert sich auf drei zentrale Themen: die Renovierung der alten Villa im Neorennaissance-Stil als Sitz der Stiftung, die Errichtung eines neuen Auditoriums und den Entwurf eines Gartens, der das Gesamtbild gliedert.

Le projet pour cette fondation médicale, issu d'un concours public en 1992, se centre autour de trois thèmes fondamentaux : la rénovation d'une ancienne villa néo-renaissance afin de pouvoir héberger le siège de la fondation, la construction d'un nouvel auditorium et le création d'un jardin articulant le tout.

El proyecto para esta fundación de medicina, ganado por concurso público en 1992, se centra en tres temas fundamentales: la renovación de una antigua villa neorrenacentista para que pueda albergar la sede de la fundación, la construcción de un nuevo auditorio y el diseño de un jardín que articule el conjunto.

Il progetto per questa fondazione medica, vinto tramite appalto pubblico nel 1992, si incentra su tre temi fondamentali: il rinnovamento di un'antica villa neorinascimentale idoneo ad ospitare la sede della fondazione, la costruzione di un nuovo auditorio e la realizzazione di un giardino che articoli tutto l'insieme.

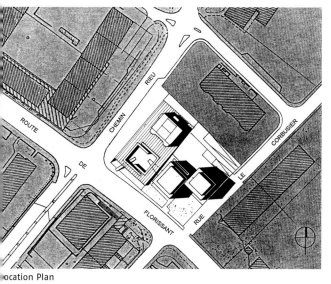

Location Plan

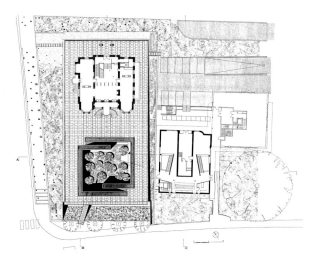

General Plan

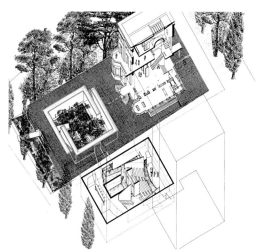

Axonometric View

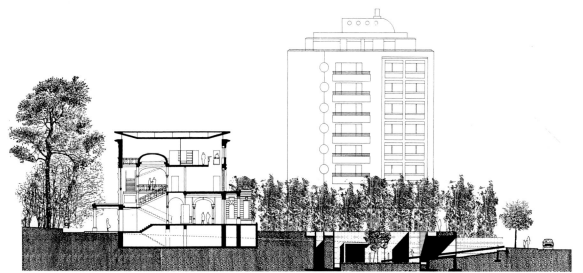

Section

Stig L. Andersson Landskabsarkitekter/SLA

Charlotte Garden

Location: Hjørring, Denmark **Completion Year:** 2003 **Photos:** © Torben Petersen

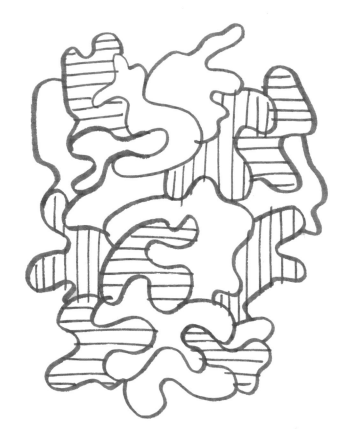

This garden, located at the center of a city block, is a reinterpretation of the traditional gardens of Northern Europe, which maintain their private character thanks to the buildings that surround them. Nevertheless, it is also open to public use, and the paths that skirt through it trace a dynamic pattern.

Dieser Garten ist eine Neuinterpretation der traditionellen Gärten Nordeuropas. Er befindet sich im Zentrum eines Häuserblocks und hat durch die umgebenden Häuser einen privaten Charakter, obwohl er gleichzeitig allen Besuchern offen steht. Die Wege, die ihn durchqueren, geben ihm ein dynamisches Muster.

Ce jardin réinterprète les jardins traditionnels du nord de l'Europe ; situé au centre d'un pâté de maisons, il conserve le caractère privé offert par la configuration des immeubles environnants mais s'ouvre, parallèlement, à l'accès public. Les tracés des sentiers le croisant dessinent un plan dynamique.

Este jardín es una reinterpretación de los jardines tradicionales del norte de Europa; situado en el centro de una manzana, conserva el carácter privado que le otorga la configuración de los edificios circundantes pero se abre, al mismo tiempo, al uso público; los trazados de los senderos que lo cruzan dibujan un patrón dinámico.

Questo giardino è una reinterpretazione dei tradizionali giardini del nord Europa; situato al centro di un isolato, conserva il carattere privato datogli dalla configurazione degli edifici circostanti ma si apre, nello stesso tempo, all'uso pubblico; i sentieri che l'attraversano presentano un tipo di tracciato dinamico.

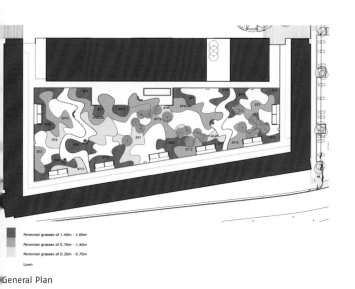

Perennial grasses of 1.40m - 2.00m
Perennial grasses of 0.70m - 1.40m
Perennial grasses of 0.20m - 0.70m
Lawn

General Plan

Sketch

CALENDAR OF PLANTING

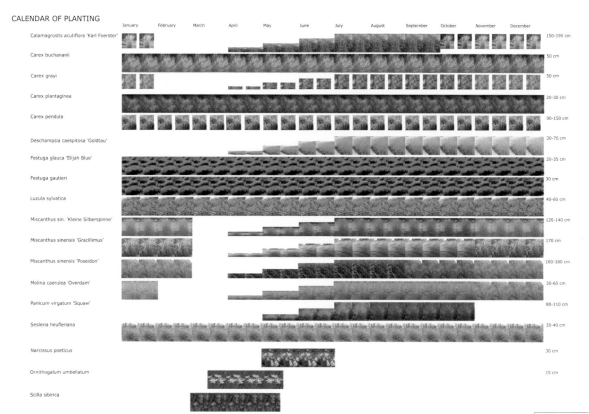

	January	February	March	April	May	June	July	August	September	October	November	December	
Calamagrostis acutiflora 'Karl Foerster'													150-190 cm
Carex buchananii													50 cm
Carex grayi													50 cm
Carex plantaginea													20-30 cm
Carex pendula													90-150 cm
Deschampsia caespitosa 'Goldtau'													30-70 cm
Festuga glauca 'Elijah Blue'													20-35 cm
Festuga gautieri													30 cm
Luzula sylvatica													40-60 cm
Miscanthus sin. 'Kleine Silberspinne'													120-140 cm
Miscanthus sinensis 'Gracillimus'													170 cm
Miscanthus sinensis 'Poseidon'													160-180 cm
Molina caerulea 'Overdam'													30-60 cm
Panicum virgatum 'Squaw'													80-110 cm
Sesleria heufleriana													30-40 cm
Narcissus poeticus													30 cm
Ornithogalum umbellatum													15 cm
Scilla sibirica													

Flowering Period Diagram

Hideki Yoshimatsu + Archipro Architects

Cemetery for the Unknown

Location: Hiroshima, Japan **Completion Year:** 2000

Photos: © Hideyuki Ashiba, Masanori Kato, Earthworks Project, Archipro Architects

The community's desire to create a memorial space that would not make any allusions to religion yielded this ephemeral and mysterious cemetery, in which 1,500 stainless steel bars make up an artificial forest in the middle of a natural setting.

Die Gemeinschaft wollte einen Ort des Gedenkens schaffen, der auf keine Religion anspielt. So entstand dieser vergänglich und geheimnisvoll wirkende Friedhof, wo 1500 Stangen aus Edelstahl einen künstlichen Wald inmitten einer natürlichen Umgebung bilden.

La volonté de la communauté de créer un espace commémoratif ne faisant allusion à aucune religion s'est accomplie dans ce cimetière à l'aspect éphémère et mystérieux, où 1.500 mâts en acier inoxydable forment un bois artificiel au cœur d'un cadre urbain.

La voluntad de la comunidad de crear un espacio conmemorativo que no aludiera a ninguna religión se fraguó en este cementerio de aspecto efímero y misterioso, donde 1.500 varas de acero inoxidable forman un bosque artificial en medio de un entorno natural.

La volontà della comunità di creare uno spazio commemorativo che non alludesse a nessuna religione si è fatto realtà in questo cimitero dall'aspetto effimero e misterioso, dove 1.500 pali di acciaio inossidabile danno vita a un bosco artificiale in mezzo a un ambiente naturale.

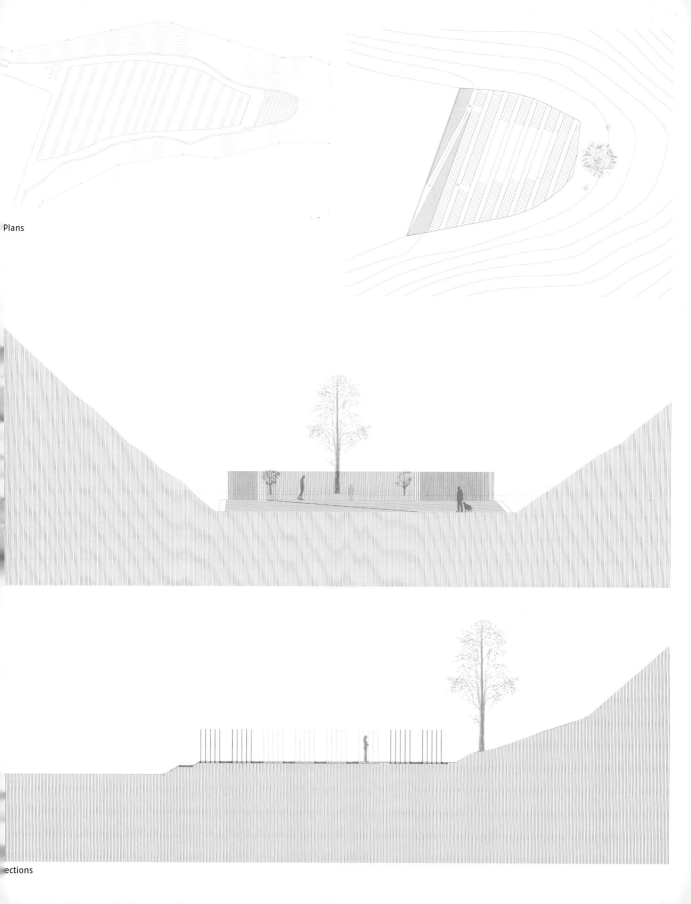

Plans

ections

Mosbach Paysagistes

Bordeaux Botanical Gardens

Location: Bordeaux, France **Completion Year:** 2002 **Photos:** © Catherine Mosbach

A modular structure that synthesizes the main characteristics of gardens—ranging from the exotic, ethno-botanic, and ecological to the contemporary—is the launching point for the composition and functionality of this project, which links the right-hand bank of the river to the historic part of the city.

Eine modulare Struktur fasst die wichtigsten Eigenschaften des Gartens – exotisch, ethnobotanisch, ökologisch und modern – zusammen. Diese Struktur ist der Ausgangspunkt für die Komposition und Funktion der Anlage, die das rechte Flussufer in den historischen Stadtkern integriert.

Une structure modulaire synthétisant les principales caractéristiques du jardin – exotique, ethnobotanique, écologique, actuel – est le point de départ de la composition et du fonctionnement du projet, qui intègre la rive droite de la rivière au centre historique de la ville.

Una estructura modular que sintetiza las principales características del jardín –exótico, etnobotánico, ecológico y actual– es el punto de partida para la composición y el funcionamiento del proyecto, que integra la margen derecha del río en el centro histórico de la ciudad.

Una struttura modulare che sintetizza le principali caratteristiche del giardino – esotico, etnobotanico, ecologico ed attuale – è il punto di partenza per la composizione e il funzionamento del progetto, che ingloba il margine destro del fiume nel centro storico della città.

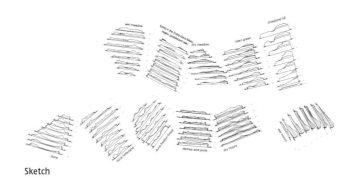

Sketch

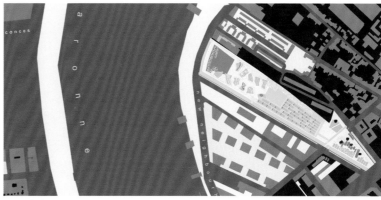

erial View

General Plan

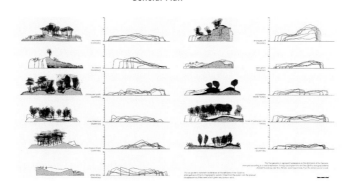

Elevations

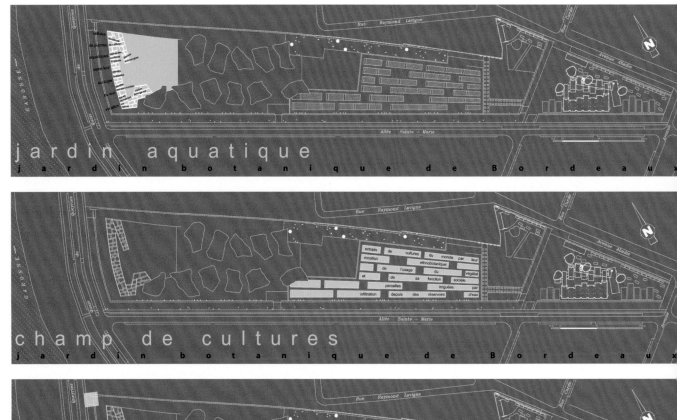

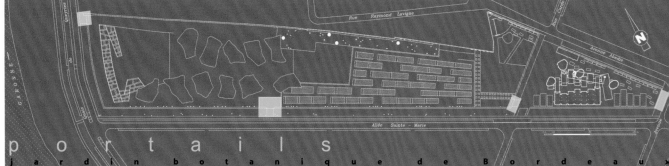

General Plan

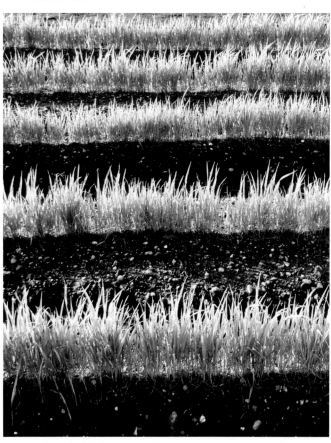

Rotzler Krebs Partner

Schönaustrasse Courtyard

Location: Basel, Switzerland **Completion Year:** 1999 **Photos:** © Ruedi Walti

A composition made up of grass rugs adorns the inner courtyard of this residential complex in Basel. The paths and play areas are marked by low, discreet fences. In the center of the plaza, varieties of maples from all over the world lend an artistic touch to the complex.

Eine Komposition aus Rasenteppichen dekoriert den Innenhof dieses Wohnkomplexes in Basel. Die Wege und Spielbereiche sind mit niedrigen, unauffälligen Zäunen abgetrennt. Im Zentrum des Platzes verleihen verschiedene Ahorne aus der ganzen Welt dem Ganzen eine künstlerische Note.

Une composition de tapis de gazon décore ce patio intérieur d'un complexe résidentiel de Bâle. Les sentiers et les aires de jeux ont été délimités par de petites haies discrètes. Au centre de la place, des variétés d'érables provenant du monde entier ajoutent une touche artistique à l'ensemble.

Una composición de alfombras de césped adorna este patio interior de un complejo residencial de Basilea. Los senderos y las zonas de juego se han delimitado con vallas bajas y discretas. En el centro de la plaza, variedades de arces provenientes de todo el mundo dan un toque artístico al conjunto.

Una composizione di tappeti erbosi adorna questo cortile interno di un complesso residenziale di Basilea. I sentieri e le zone di gioco sono stati delimitati con steccati bassi e discreti. Al centro della piazza, diverse varietà di aceri provenienti da tutto il mondo danno un tocco artistico a tutto l'insieme.

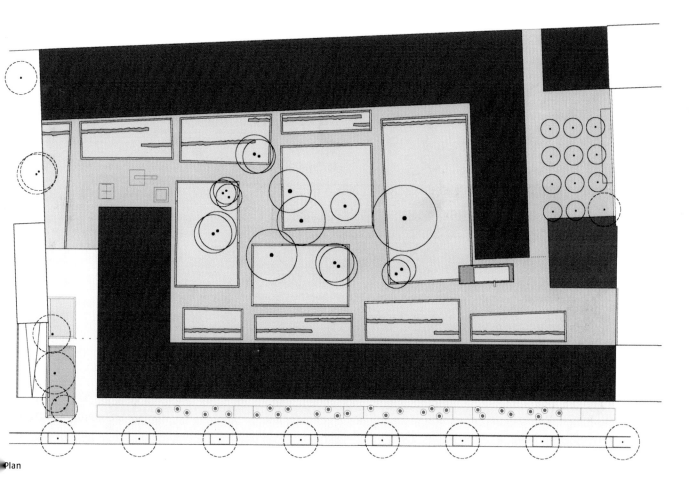

Plan

Taylor Cullity Lethlean

North Terrace

Location: Adelaide, Australia **Completion Year:** 2005 **Photos:** © Grant Hancock, Emily Taylor

The most emblematic buildings of the city, such as the library, the botanical garden, museums, galleries, universities, and the parliament are located along North Terrace Boulevard. This linear garden was designed to emphasize the importance of this civic and cultural axis of the city.

An dem North Terrace Boulevard befinden sich die bedeutendsten Gebäude der Stadt wie die Bibliothek, der botanische Garten, Museen, Galerien, Universitäten und das Parlament. Dieser lineare Garten wurde entworfen, um die Bedeutung dieser bürgerlichen und kulturellen Achse der Stadt zu unterstreichen.

Les édifices les plus emblématiques, ainsi la bibliothèque, le jardin botanique, les musées, galeries, universités et le Parlement, s'invitent tout au long du boulevard de North Terrace. Ce jardin linéaire a été pensé pour souligner l'importance de cet axe civique et culturel de la ville.

A lo largo del bulvar North Terrace se ubican los edificios más emblemáticos de la ciudad, como la biblioteca, el jardín botánico, museos, galerías, universidades y el parlamento. Este jardín lineal ha sido diseñado para subrayar la importancia de este eje cívico y cultural de la ciudad.

Lungo il boulevard North Terrace si trovano gli edifici più emblematici della città, come la biblioteca, il giardino botanico, i musei, le gallerie, le università e il parlamento. Questo giardino lineare è stato disegnato per sottolineare l'importanza di questo asse urbano e culturale della città.

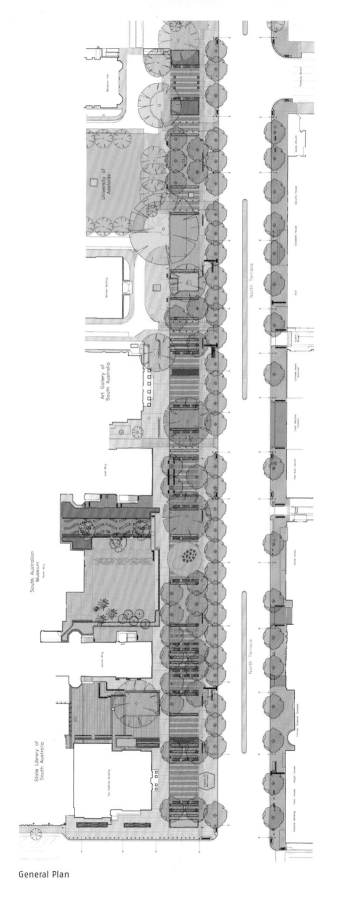

General Plan

Karres en Brands

Berestein Cemetery

Location: 's-Graveland, Netherlands Completion Year: 2000

Photos: © Karres en Brands, Peter van Bolhuis/Pandion

The intervention in this 17th-century cemetery aimed to spawn a relationship between the existing zones and a series of new structures, through axes that would emphasize the contrasts between the remnants from different eras and would bring out the gardens to their fullest.

Bei den Eingriffen auf diesem alten Friedhof aus dem 17. Jh. wurde eine Beziehung zwischen den bestehenden Bereichen und den neuen Strukturen geschaffen. Dies geschah mithilfe von Achsen, die den Kontrast zwischen den verschiedenen Epochen unterstreichen und die Gärten bestmöglich okzentuieren.

L'intervention dans cet ancien cimetière XVIIème supposait la création d'une relation entre les zones existantes et les nouvelles structures grâce à des axes mettant en relief les contrastes entre les différentes époques et tirant le meilleur parti des jardins.

La intervención en este antiguo cementerio del siglo XVII suponía crear una relación entre las zonas existentes y las nuevas estructuras mediante ejes que enfatizaran los contrastes entre las diferentes épocas y sacaran el mayor partido a los jardines.

L'intervento in questo antico cimitero del XVII secolo supponeva creare un rapporto tra le zone esistenti e le nuove strutture mediante assi che enfatizzassero i contrasti tra le diverse epoche e traessero il maggior vantaggio dai giardini.

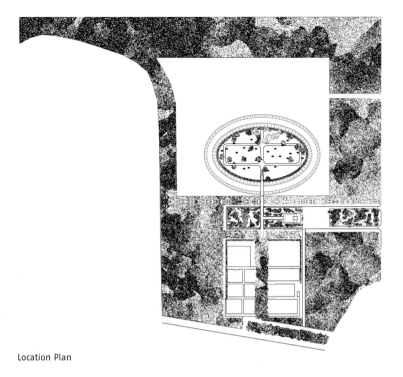

Location Plan

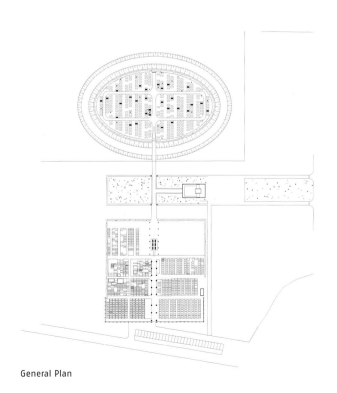

General Plan

Janet Rosenberg & Associates, Quadrangle

30 Adelaide Street East

Location: Toronto, Canada Completion Year: 2002 Photos: © Neil Fox

This small public garden functions as the atrium of a recently-renovated office building in downtown Toronto. So as to create an intimate space, the formal language of the building was revisited, and the same materials were used in the construction of the garden.

Dieser kleine öffentliche Garten dient als Atrium für ein Bürogebäude im Zentrum von Toronto, das vor kurzem renoviert wurde. Um eine intime Umgebung zu schaffen, wurde die formale Sprache des Gebäudes wieder aufgenommen sowie die gleichen Materialien verwendet, die schon für den Bau benutzt wurden.

Ce petit jardin public fonctionne comme un atrium pour un immeuble de bureaux récemment rénové du centre de Toronto. Afin de créer un espace intime, le langage formel de l'édifice a été repris de même que les matériaux employés pour sa construction.

Este pequeño jardín público funciona como atrio de un edificio de oficinas recientemente renovado en el centro de Toronto. Para crear un espacio íntimo se retoma el lenguaje formal del edificio y se emplean los mismos materiales que se usaron para su construccción.

Questo piccolo giardino pubblico funge da atrio di un edificio di uffici recentemente rinnovato nel centro di Toronto. Per creare uno spazio intimo, si riprende il linguaggio formale dell'edificio e si utilizzano gli stessi materiali adoperati per la sua costruzione.

ASPECT Landscape Architecture

Five Dock Square

Location: Sydney, Australia **Completion Year:** 2004 **Photos:** © Sacha Coles

This group of buildings, which houses residences, a supermarket, and a public library, is arranged around a central garden patio where several skylights provide the library with natural light.

Diese Gebäudegruppe, in der sich ein Supermarkt, eine öffentliche Bibliothek und Wohnungen befinden, steht um einen begrünten Innenhof, zu dem sich Fenster öffnen, durch die Licht in die Bibliothek fällt.

Cet ensemble d'immeubles, accueillant un supermarché, une bibliothèque publique et des logements, s'organise autour d'un patio central sur lequel s'ouvrent des lucernaires éclairant la bibliothèque.

Este conjunto de edificios, que alberga un supermercado, una biblioteca pública y viviendas, se organiza alrededor de un patio central ajardinado hacia donde se abren unos lucernarios que proporcionan luz a la biblioteca.

Questo complesso di edifici, che comprende un supermercato, una biblioteca pubblica e delle abitazioni, si struttura attorno a un cortile centrale con piante su cui si affacciano i lucernari che forniscono luce alla biblioteca.

oslund.and.assoc.

General Mills Corporate

Location: Golden Valley, MN, USA **Completion Year:** 2004 **Photos:** © George Heinrich, Tadd Kreun

The design for this project—which dates from 1950 and was drafted by Skidmore, Owings and Merrill—needed to be brought up to date, both to serve the complex's new needs and to integrate the newer buildings that had been added since. Hence, a continuous green space was created, on top of which the buildings delicately rise.

Das Originalprojekt aus dem Jahr 1950, das von dem Studio Skidmore, Owings and Merrill geplant wurde, sollte an die neuen Anforderungen innerhalb des Komplexes angepasst und eine Reihe von angefügten Gebäuden mussten integriert werden. Man schuf eine durchgehende Grünzone, in die Gebäude sensibel eingebettet sind.

Le projet original de 1950, conçu par le cabinet Skidmore, Owings and Merrill, devait s'adapter aux nouveaux impératifs du complexe et intégrer à l'ensemble des immeubles s'ajoutant par la suite. Un espace vert continu vit alors le jour, sur lequel s'appuient délicatement les édifices.

El proyecto original de 1950, diseñado por el estudio Skidmore, Owings and Merrill, debía adecuarse a las nuevas necesidades del complejo e integrar en el conjunto los edificios que se fueran añadiendo. Se creó entonces una zona verde continua donde se apoyan delicadamente los edificios.

Il progetto originale del 1950, disegnato dallo studio Skidmore, Owings and Merrill, doveva adeguarsi alle nuove esigenze del complesso e integrare in tutto l'insieme gli edifici che man mano venivano costruiti. Si creò pertanto una zona verde continua sulla quale si adagiano delicatamente gli edifici.

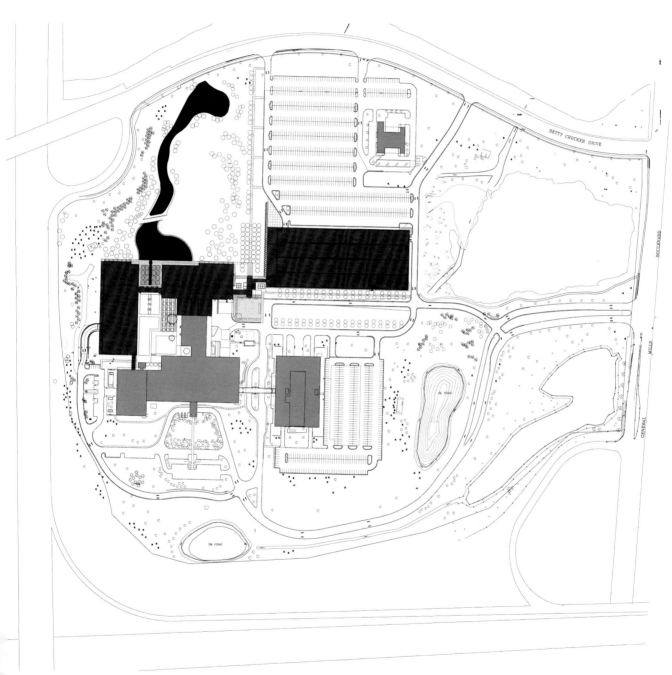

General Plan

Taylor Cullity Lethlean

Forest Gallery

Location: Carlton, Australia **Completion Year:** 2000 **Photos:** © Ben Wrigley, Carla Gottgens

Located in a spacious inner courtyard, at Victoria's New Museum, the Forest Gallery is a faithful reproduction of the forests on Mount Ash, located to the east of the city. This space recreates a natural environment, which is monitored using the latest in technology.

In einem großen Innenhof des neuen Museums von Victoria befindet sich die Forest Gallery, eine originalgetreue Nachbildung der Wälder auf dem Berg Ash im Osten der Stadt. Hier wird eine natürliche Umgebung nachgestellt, die mit komplizierttester Technologie kontrolliert wird.

Située dans un vaste patio intérieur du nouveau musée de Victoria, la Forest Gallery est une reproduction fidèle des bois du mont Ash, se trouvant à l'est de la ville. L'espace recrée une atmosphère naturelle contrôlée avec la technologie la plus sophistiquée.

Ubicada en un amplio patio interior del nuevo museo de Victoria, la Forest Galleryes una fiel reproducción de los bosques del monte Ash, situado al este de la ciudad. El espacio recrea un ambiente natural que se controla con la más sofisticada tecnología.

Situata in un ampio cortile interno del nuovo museo di Victoria, la Forest Gallery è una fedele riproduzione dei boschi del monte Ash, ad est della città. Lo spazio ricrea un ambiente naturale controllato mediante la più sofisticata tecnologia.

Daniela Mongini, Gianna Attiani/LAND-I

Mente la-menta?

Location: Chaumont-sur-Loire, France Completion Year: 2000 Photos: © LAND-I

La fumeé

Le radeau

L'eau

The word play in the title of this ephemeral work encompasses the two fundamental questions posed by the design: "does the mind mind?" (mente la menta?) Can we be sure that our natural resources will resist our predatory exploitation? And does the mind lament (mente lamenta?)? Do our minds suffer as a result of this situation, and are we conscious of it?

Das Wortspiel im Namen dieses flüchtigen Werkes fasst die beiden grundlegenden Fragen zusammen, die bei dieser Planung gestellt wurden, die nach der Natur und unserer Situation. Gespielt wurde mit den Begriffen mente, menta und lamenta, also Geist, Minze, lügen und klagen. Lügt die Minze, ist die Minze der Geist? Können wir uns darauf verlassen, dass die natürlichen Ressourcen uns widerstehen können? Und beklagt sich der Geist? Leiden wir unter unserer Situation? Sind wir uns darüber bewusst?

Le jeu de mot du titre de cet œuvre éphémère résume les deux questions fondamentales posées par le projet : d'une part, la menthe ment-elle (« mente la menta ? ») ? Sommes-nous certains que les ressources naturelles peuvent résister à notre exploitation prédatrice ? Et de l'autre, la menthe se lamente-t-elle (« mente lamenta ? ») ? Notre esprit souffre-t-il de cette situation ? En sommes-nous conscients ?

El juego de palabras del título de esta obra efímera resume las dos cuestiones fundamentales que plantea el proyecto: por una parte, ¿miente la menta? ("mente la menta?") ¿Estamos seguros de que los recursos naturales pueden resistir nuestra explotación depredadora? Y por otra, ¿se queja la mente?" ("mente lamenta?") ¿Sufre nuestra mente por esta situación? ¿Somos conscientes de ello?

Il gioco di parole del titolo di quest'opera effimera riassume le due questioni fondamentali che pone il progetto: da una parte, "mente la menta"? Siamo sicuri che le risorse naturali possono resistere al nostro sfruttamento depredatore? E dall'altra, "mente lamenta"? Soffre la nostra mente per questa situazione? Ne siamo consapevoli?

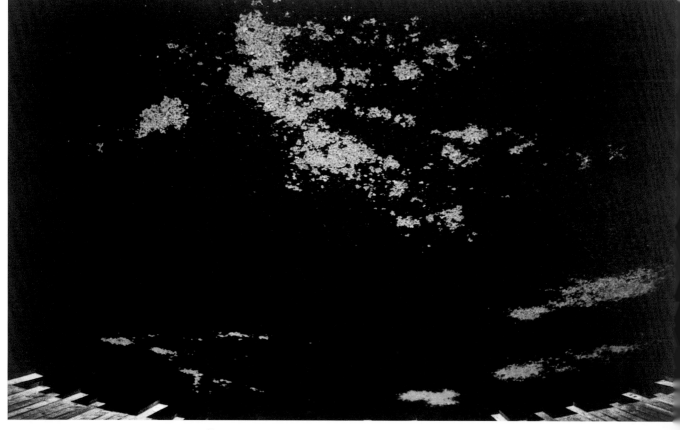

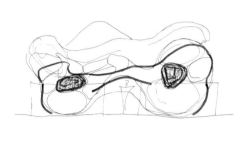

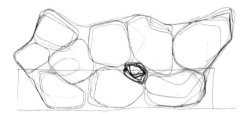

Sketches

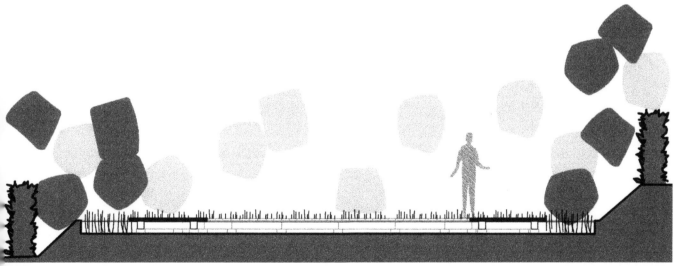

etail Section

Levin Monsigny Landschaftsarchitekten

Academy Plaza

Location: Berlin, Germany **Completion Year:** 2004 **Photos:** © Claas Dreppenstedt

This plaza forms part of a vast public space in the neighborhood of Adlershof, which houses a major community of researchers and scientists. The ground was paved in the same materials as were used to build the historical buildings in the surrounding area.

Dieser Platz gehört zu einer großen, öffentlichen Anlage im Viertel Adlershof, dem modernen Wissenschafts- und Forschungsstandort Berlins. Der Platz wurde mit dem gleichen Material gepflastert, das für den Bau der umgebenden historischen Gebäude verwand wurde.

Cette place fait partie d'un vaste espace public du quartier d'Adlershof, abritant une importante communauté dédiée à la science et à la recherche. Le revêtement a vu l'utilisation des mêmes matériaux que ceux des bâtiments historiques avoisinants.

Esta plaza forma parte de un vasto espacio público del barrio de Adlershof, que alberga una importante comunidad dedicada a la ciencia y a la investigación. Para la pavimentación se usaron los mismos materiales con que se construyeron los edificios históricos que la rodean.

Questa piazza fa parte di un vasto spazio pubblico del quartiere di Adlershof, dove nel 1991 è sorta l'importante città della scienza e della ricerca. Per la pavimentazione sono stati usati gli stessi materiali adoperati per costruire gli storici edifici che circondano la piazza.

General Plan

Rotzler Krebs Partner

VP Bank

Location: Vaduz, Principality of Liechtenstein **Completion Year:** 2004 **Photos:** © Rotzler Krebs Partner

This plaza serves as an atrium and green area for VP Bank's office complex. Granite flagstones are topped by a large, rectangular planter, while a series of steel containers—reminiscent of ponds—store reserves of water for watering the plants.

Dieser Platz dient als Atrium und Grünzone für einen Bürokomplex der VP Bank. Auf einer Pflasterung aus Granitplatten steht ein großer rechteckiger Blumenbehälter, und in Stahlcontainern in Form von Wasserbassins wird Wasser zum Gießen gespeichert.

Cette place servait d'atrium et de zone verte au complexe de bureaux de la VP Bank. À un revêtement de plaques de granit se superpose une grande jardinière rectangulaire ; des conteneurs d'acier en forme d'étang emmagasinent l'eau pour l'arrosage.

Esta plaza sirve de atrio y zona verde al complejo de oficinas de la VP Bank. A un pavimento de placas de granito se superpone una gran jardinera rectangular; unos contenedores de acero con forma de estanque almacenan el agua para el riego.

Questa piazza serve da atrio e zona verde al complesso di uffici della VP Bank. A un pavimento in lastre di granito si sovrappone una gran fioriera; l'acqua per annaffiare il prato e i fiori viene accumulata in dei contenitori di acciaio a forma di laghetto.

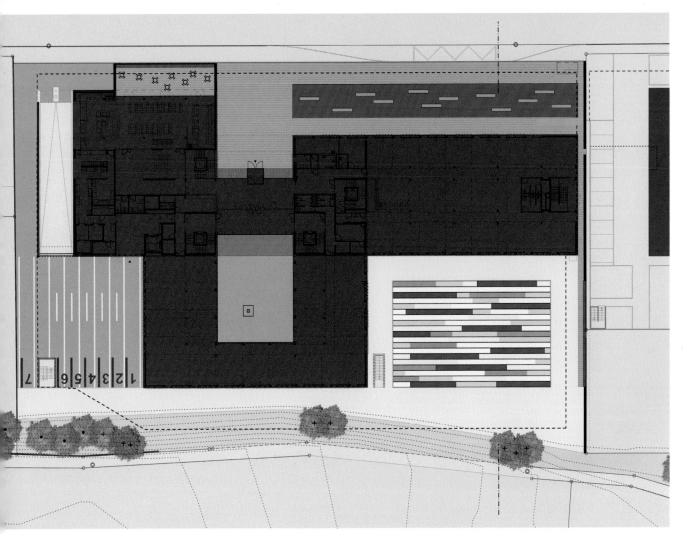

General Plan

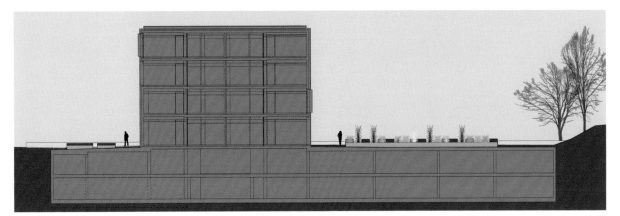

Section

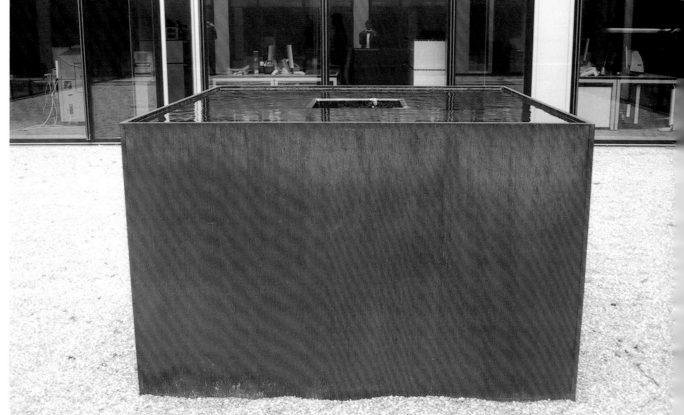

Raderschall Landschaftsarchitekten

Innenhof Westpark

Location: Zurich, Switzerland **Completion Year:** 2002 **Photos:** © Markus Fierz, Philipp Rohner

The narrow dimensions of the inner courtyard of this office building determined the character of this project: a three-dimensional garden. A framework of flowers emphasizes the rectangular shape of the site, while a taut wire that stretches to the fourth floor of the building allows the garden to extend upward.

Die engen Proportionen des Innenhofs dieses Bürogebäudes bestimmten den Charakter dieses Gartens, der in drei Dimensionen angelegt wurde. Ein Rahmen aus Blumen unterstreicht die rechteckige Form, und über ein Kabel, das bis zum vierten Stock des Gebäudes gespannt wurde, können die Pflanzen in die Vertikale wachsen.

Les proportions réduites du patio intérieur de cet immeuble de bureaux ont déterminé le caractère du projet : un jardin en trois dimensions. Un cadre floral souligne la forme rectangulaire de l'endroit alors qu'un câble tendu provenant du quatrième étage de l'édifice permet au jardin de se prolonger à la verticale.

Las estrechas proporciones del patio interior de este edificio de oficinas determinaron el carácter del proyecto; un jardín en tres dimensiones. Un marco de flores subraya la forma rectangular del recinto mientras que un cable tensado que llega a la cuarta planta del edificio permite que el jardín se extienda en vertical.

Le strette proporzioni del cortile interno di questo edificio di uffici hanno determinato il carattere del progetto; un giardino a tre dimensioni. Una cornice di fiori sottolinea la forma rettangolare del recinto mentre un cavo teso che arriva fino al quarto piano dell'edificio consente al giardino di estendersi in verticale.

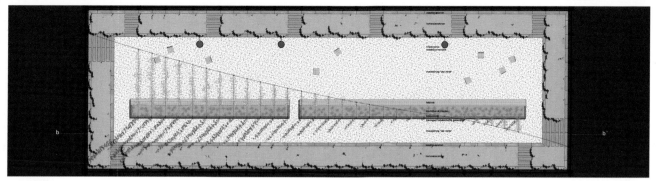

General Plan

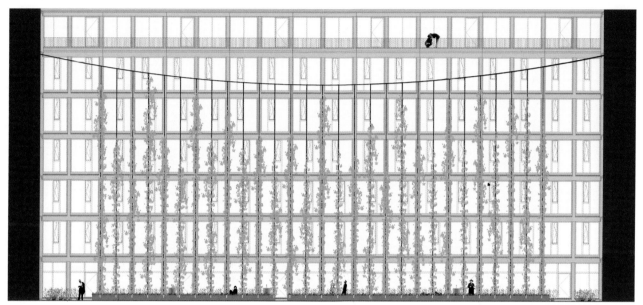

Longitudinal Section

Cross Section

Landworks Studio

Court Square
Press Building

Location: Boston, MA, USA **Completion Year:** 2004 **Photos:** © Landworks Studio

The small dimensions of the patio and the fragmented view caused by the windows of the building characterize the design of this garden. Basic elements of the design are its asymmetric forms, varied vegetation, and suggestive lighting.

Der Innenhof ist sehr klein und die Aussicht aus den Fenstern des Gebäudes stark unterteilt, was die Gestaltung dieses Gartens ausschlaggebend beeinflusst hat. Asymmetrische Formen mit einer abwechslungsreichen Vegetation und eine faszinierende Beleuchtung waren die grundlegenden Gestaltungselemente.

Les proportions réduites du patio et la vision fragmentée offerte par les fenêtres de l'édifice ont marqué le design de ce jardin. Formes asymétriques, végétation variée, illumination suggestive sont les éléments essentiels du design.

Las reducidas proporciones del patio y la visión fragmentada que ofrecían las ventanas del edificio marcaron el diseño de este jardín. Formas asimétricas, una variada vegetación y una iluminación sugerente son los elementos básicos del diseño.

Le ridotte proporzioni del cortile e la vista frammentata che offrivano le finestre dell'edificio hanno condizionato il disegno di questo giardino. Tra gli elementi principali: forme asimmetriche, una vegetazione alquanto varia e una suggestiva illuminazione.

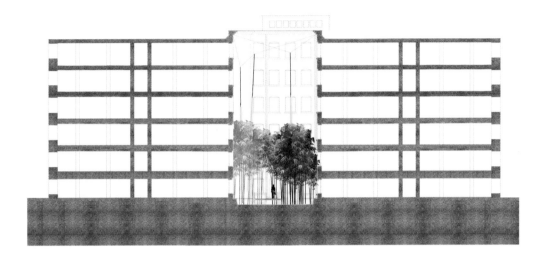

Cross Section

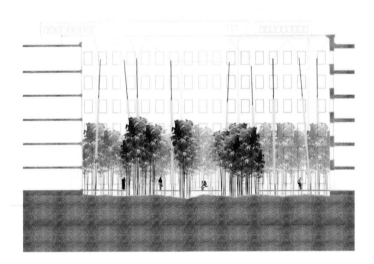

Longitudinal Section

ASPECT Landscape Architecture

National Emergency Services Memorial

Location: Canberra, Australia   Completion Year: 2004   Photos: © Ben Wrigley

This monument is located on the important Anzac Parade Avenue in the Australian capital, where the city's most important civic buildings and monuments are located. Its design creates a dialogue with the surrounding historic buildings, and at the same time it acts as a counterpoint to the strict symmetry of the esplanade.

Dieses Monument steht an der eindrucksvollen Allee Anzac Parade in der Hauptstadt Australiens, an der sich die wichtigsten zivilen Gebäude und Monumente der Stadt befinden. Das Denkmal ist so entworfen, dass es mit den umgebenden historischen Gebäuden im Dialog steht und gleichzeitig einen Gegensatz zu der strengen Symmetrie der Esplanade schafft.

Le monument se situe sur l'imposante avenue Anzac Parade, dans la capitale australienne, qui compte les immeubles civique et les monuments les plus importants de la ville. Le design de cette pièce dialogue avec les bâtiments historiques qui l'entourent et, simultanément, offre un contrepoint à la symétrie stricte de l'esplanade.

El monumento se emplaza en la imponente avenida Anzac Parade, en la capital australiana, que cuenta con los más importantes edificios cívicos y monumentos de la ciudad. El diseño de esta pieza dialoga con los edificios históricos que la rodean y al mismo tiempo hace de contrapunto a la estricta simetría de la explanada.

Il monumento sorge nel viale Anzac Parade, imponente arteria della capitale australiana dove si susseguono gli edifici civili e i monumenti più importanti della città. Le sue linee dialogano con quelle degli edifici storici che lo circondano e allo stesso tempo fa da contrappunto alla rigida simmetria della spianata.

service humility
camaraderie trust capability
awe vulnerability spirit grief sacrifice courage skill com

vice humility v olunte

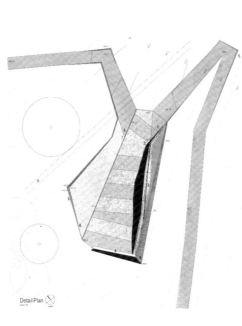

Detail Plan

General Plan

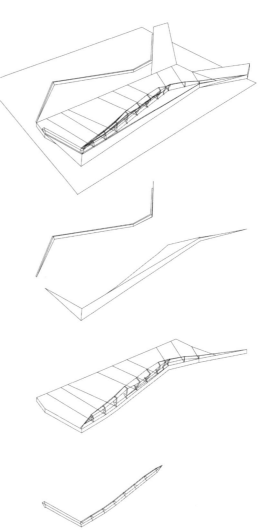

Structure Diagrams

vigilance preparation service humility volunteerism prevention cooperation camaraderie trust adaptability awe vulnerability spirit grief sacrifice courage skill compassion support honour celebration recovery humanity community hope

evations

5/2 6

West 8

Expo '02

Collaborators: Diller & Scofidio

Location: Yverdon-les-Bains, Switzerland **Completion Year:** 2002 **Photos:** © Jeroen Musch

Here, the area surrounding the pavilions on a fairground had to be remodeled to reflect the theme "Human Sensuality". This design, which combines lively colors and psychedelic patterns, transforms the nearby hills into a surrealist landscape.

Die Umgebung der Messehallen sollte so umgestaltet werden, dass dem Ausstellungsthema „Menschliche Sinnlichkeit" entsprochen wurde. In der Gestaltung wurden kräftige Farben und psychedelische Muster verwendet, so dass aus den umgebenden Hügeln eine surrealistische Landschaft wurde.

L'environnement adjacent aux pavillons de l'exposition devait être rénové en suivant le thème de l'exposition « Sensualité humaine ». Le design, conjuguant couleurs vivaces et formes psychédéliques, transforme les collines environnantes en un paysage surréaliste.

El entorno adyacente a los pabellones de la feria debía ser remodelado siguiendo el tema de la exposición "Sensualidad humana". El diseño, que conjuga colores vivaces y patrones psicodélicos, transforma las colinas circundantes en un paisaje surrealista.

La zona attorno ai padiglioni della fiera doveva essere ristrutturata seguendo il tema della mostra "Sensualità umana". Il progetto decorativo, che coniuga colori vivaci e modelli psichedelici, trasforma le colline circostanti in un paesaggio surrealista.

Janet Rosenberg & Associates

Harmony of Opposites

Location: Ottawa, Canada Completion Year: 2001 Photos: © Johnathan Hayward

The aesthetic behind this booth for the Canadian Tulip Festival, where participants aim to display tulips in the most original way possible, is inspired by the patterns found in the Dutch landscape, the paintings of Piet Mondrian, and the sculptures of Claes Oldenburg and Coosje van Bruggen.

Dieses Büro für das Canadian Tulip Festival, auf dem Tulpen so originell wie möglich ausgestellt werden sollten, ist von den Mustern der holländischen Blumenfelder, von den Bildern Piet Mondrians und den Skulpturen von Claes Oldenburg und Coosje van Bruggen inspiriert.

L'esthétique de ce bureau pour le Canadian Tulip Festival, dont l'objectif est d'exposer des tulipes de la manière la plus originale, s'inspire de la physionomie de la campagne hollandaise dans la peinture de Piet Mondrian et les sculptures de Claes Oldenburg et Coosje van Bruggen.

La estética de este despacho para el Canadian Tulip Festival, cuyo objetivo es exhibir tulipanes de la manera más original, se inspira en los patrones del campo holandés, en las pinturas de Piet Mondrian y en las esculturas de Claes Oldenburg y Coosje van Bruggen.

L'estetica di questo ufficio per il Canadian Tulip Festival, il cui obiettivo è l'esposizione originale di tulipani, si inspira ai modelli della campagna olandese, ai dipinti di Piet Mondrian e alle sculture di Claes Oldenburg e Coosje van Bruggen.

AN EVENTFUL PATH

This installation was inspired by the intense festivity at Sydney Olympic Park created by events such as the Sydney 2000 Olympic Games, Paralympic Games and the 2003 Rugby World Cup. The composition of coloured glass symbolises the many components required to stage international events of this scale. The linear path is an abstract timeline celebrating the past and leading towards the future. This installation will evolve over time with the inscription of bronze plaques to commemorate new major events held at Sydney Olympic Park. At night, the path illuminates. This way lies the Park's major events precinct.

DESIGNED BY ASPECT STUDIO IN COLLABORATION WITH FLEDER ASSOCIATES

Aspect Landscape Architecture

The Eventful Path

Collaborators: Feeder Associates Graphic Designers

Location: Sydney, Australia **Completion Year:** 2004 **Photos:** © Ross Honeysett

SYDNEY 2000
OLYMPIC GAMES

This 145 foot long installation commemorates the sporting and cultural events that took place in the Sydney Olympic Park. The setting is a composition of colored glass blocks, a stainless steel canal, fluorescent lights, and polished concrete pavement.

Diese 45 Meter lange Anlage erinnert an die kulturellen und sportlichen Veranstaltungen, die im Sydney Olympic Park stattgefunden haben. Das gesamte Ensemble setzt sich zusammen aus Blöcken aus buntem Glas, einem Kanal aus Edelstahl, Leuchtstoffröhren und Böden aus poliertem Zement.

Cette installation de 45 m de long commémore les événements culturels et sportifs célébrés au Sydney Olympic Park. Des blocs de verre de couleurs, un canal en acier inoxydable, des lumières fluorescentes et un revêtement de béton lissé sont les éléments composant l'ensemble.

Esta instalación, de 45 m de largo, conmemora los eventos culturales y deportivos que se celebraron en el Sydney Olympic Park. Bloques de cristal de colores, un canal de acero inoxidable, luces fluorescentes y un pavimento de hormigón pulido son los elementos que componen el conjunto.

Questa installazione, lunga 45 m, commemora gli eventi culturali e sportivi tenutisi nel Sydney Olympic Park. Ne fanno parte blocchi di vetro colorati, un canale in acciaio inossidabile, luci fluorescenti e un pavimento in cemento levigato.

RUGBY
WORLD
CUP

10.10.03 / 22.11.03

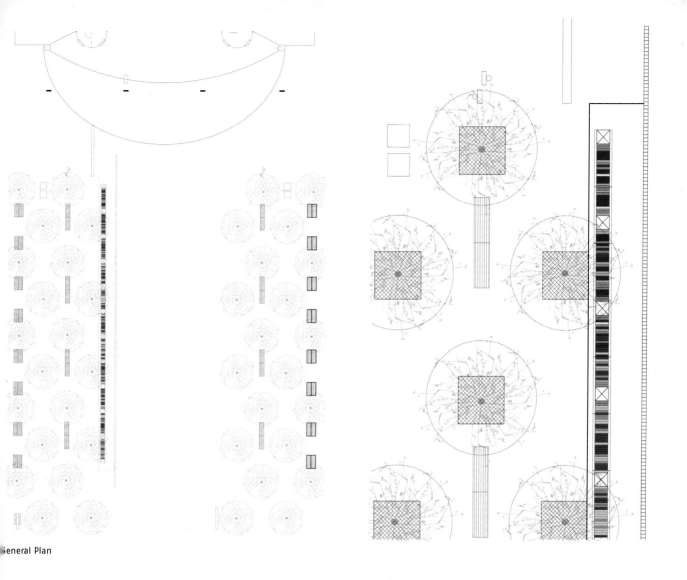

General Plan

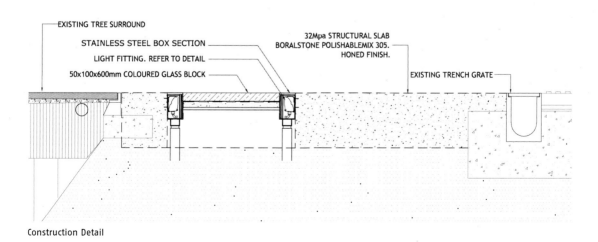

EXISTING TREE SURROUND

STAINLESS STEEL BOX SECTION

LIGHT FITTING. REFER TO DETAIL

50x100x600mm COLOURED GLASS BLOCK

32Mpa STRUCTURAL SLAB
BORALSTONE POLISHABLEMIX 305.
HONED FINISH.

EXISTING TRENCH GRATE

Construction Detail

ASPECT Landscape Architecture

Car Park

Location: Sydney, Australia Completion Year: 2004 Photos: © Sacha Coles, Simon Wood

This installation, created for the Garden Exhibition in the Royal Botanical Garden in Sydney, takes a whimsical look at certain aspects of contemporary landscape design, such as the role of the automobile, the influence of parking lots around urban areas, and the creation of artificial landscapes.

Diese Anlage, die für die Garden Exhibition im Royal Botanical Garden in Sydney geschaffen wurde, analysiert auf humorvolle Weise einige Aspekte des heutigen Landschaftsdesigns, wie die Rolle des Autos, der Einfluss der Parkplätze auf die städtischen Umgebungen und die Schaffung von künstlichen Landschaften.

Cette installation, créée dans le cadre de la Garden Exhibition du Royal Botanical Garden de Sydney, analyse, avec un regard amusé, quelques aspects du design du paysage actuel. Le rôle de l'automobile, l'influence des zones de stationnement dans les environnements urbains et la création de paysages artificiels.

Esta instalación, creada con motivo de la Garden Exhibition en el Royal Botanical Garden de Sydney, analiza, con una mirada divertida, unos aspectos del diseño del paisaje actual. El papel del automóvil, la influencia de las zonas de aparcamiento en los entornos urbanos y la creación de paisajes artificiales.

Questa installazione, creata in occasione della Garden Exhibition nel Royal Botanical Garden di Sydney, analizza, con uno sguardo ameno alcuni aspetti che caratterizzano il paesaggio attuale. Il ruolo dell'automobile, l'influenza delle zone di parcheggio nelle aree urbane e la creazione di paesaggi artificiali.

NIP paysage

trans[plant]

Location: Ottawa, Canada Completion Year: 2002 Photos: © NIP Paysage, Hans Blohm

This project, a temporary garden installation at the Canadian Tulip Festival, is an homage to Princess Margaret, one of the festival's promoters. An elongated, narrow bed of tulips is a tiny fragment of the Dutch landscape, but in Canada. Of especial importance are the tulip bulbs, which float in glass tubes.

Diese Anlage ist eine Hommage an die Prinzessin Margarita, die das Canadian Tulip Festival förderte, für das dieser temporäre Garten geschaffen wurde. Ein langes, enges Tulpenbeet stellt einen Ausschnitt der holländischen Landschaft in Kanada dar. Besonderes Augenmerk wurde auf die Tulpenzwiebeln gerichtet, die in Kristallrohren schweben.

Le projet rend hommage à la princesse Margaret, marraine du Canadian Tulip Festival, où s'est installé ce jardin temporaire. Un lit allongé et étroit de tulipes se propose en fragment de paysage hollandais au Canada. Une importance toute spéciale a été accordée aux bulbes, flottant dans des tubes en verre.

El proyecto rinde homenaje a la princesa Margarita, promotora del Canadian Tulip Festival, donde se instaló este jardín temporal. Un alargado y estrecho lecho de tulipanes es un fragmento de paisaje holandés en Canadá. Especial importancia se le ha dado a los bulbos, que flotan en tubos de cristal.

Il progetto rende omaggio alla principessa Margherita, promotrice del Canadian Tulip Festival, dove è stato installato questo giardino temporaneo. Un lungo e stretto letto di tulipani rappresenta un frammento di paesaggio olandese in Canada. Particolare importanza è stata data ai bulbi, che galleggiano in tubi di vetro.

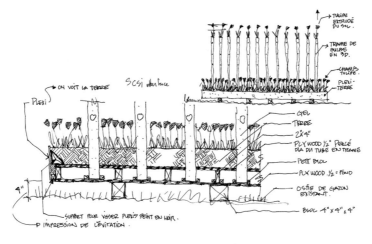

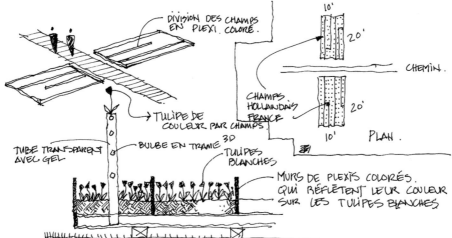

Sketches

Elevations

Populus tremuloïde
Peuplier faux-trembl
Trembling aspen
H:25m Dia:40cm Longé

NIP paysage

In Vitro

Location: Métis, Canada **Completion Year:** 2001 **Photos:** © Michel Laverdière, Jean-Claude Hurni

This garden, installed for the International Festival of Gardens, is an attempt to update the traditional vision of a forest. The role that a forest plays in today's society (as a cultural reference, industrial resource, and a place for pleasure) is recreated with urban and contemporary elements.

Dieser Garten, angelegt für das International Festival of Gardens, ist ein Versuch, die traditionelle Auffassung des Waldes auf den neuesten Stand zu bringen und zu visualisieren. Die Rolle des Waldes in der heutigen Gesellschaft – kulturelle Referenz, industrielle Ressourcen und Ort für Freizeitvergnügungen – wird mit städtischen und zeitgenössischen Elementen nachgeahmt.

Ce jardin, installé pour l'International Festival of Gardens, est un essai d'actualisation de la vision traditionnelle du bois. Les fonctions remplies par le bois dans la société actuelle (référent culturel, ressource industrielle, lieu de plaisir) sont recréées avec des éléments urbains et contemporains.

Este jardín, instalado para el International Festival of Gardens, es un intento de actualizar la visión tradicional del bosque. Los papeles que desempeña el bosque en la sociedad actula (referente cultural, recurso industrial, lugar de placer) se recrean con elementos urbanos y contemporáneos.

Questo giardino, allestito per l'International Festival of Gardens, è un tentativo di aggiornare la visione tradizionale del bosco. I ruoli svolti dal bosco nella società attuale (referente culturale, risorsa industriale, luogo di svago e riposo) vengono ricreati mediante elementi urbani e contemporanei.

Elevation

NIP paysage

Flood Garden

Location: Chaumont-sur-Loire, France **Completion Year:** 1998 **Photos:** © Édith Julien

A garden commemorating the floods of the Saguenay region in Québec in 1996 was the starting point for this unique project. Objects from daily life such as chairs, tables, stairs, float half sunken in the terrain and invite the visitor to explore this fantasy garden.

Ein Garten, der an die Überschwemmungen in der Region Saguenay in Québec im Jahr 1996 erinnert, war der Ausgangspunkt für dieses außerordentliche Projekt. Objekte des täglichen Lebens wie Stühle, Tische, Leitern, fließen halb vergraben im Gelände und laden den Besucher zum Eintritt in diesen Fantasiegarten ein.

Un jardin commémorant les inondations de la région de Saguenay an Québec en 1996 est le point de départ de la réalisation de ce projet singulier. Éléments de la vie quotidienne, chaises, tables, escaliers, flottent à demi immergés dans le terrain et invitent le visiteur à s'aventurer dans ce jardin extraordinaire.

Un jardín que conmemorara las inundaciones de la región de Saguenay en Québec en 1996 ha sido el punto de partida para realizar este singular proyecto. Elementos de la vida cotidiana, sillas, mesas, escaleras, flotan semihundidos en el terreno e invitan al visitante a adentrarse en este jardín de fantasía.

Un giardino che commemora le inondazioni della regione di Saguenay, in Quebec, avvenute nel 1996, è stato il punto di partenza per realizzare questo singolare progetto. Elementi della vita quotidiana, sedie, tavoli, scale, galleggiano semi-infossati nel terreno e invitano il visitatore ad addentrarsi in questo giardino di fantasia.

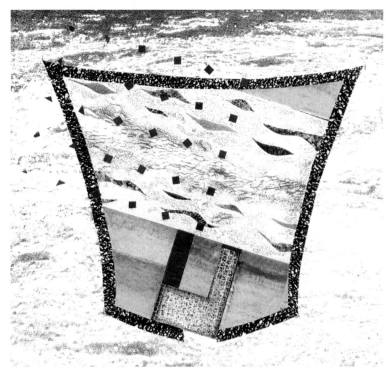

General Plan

Claude Cormier Architectes Paysagistes

Solange

Location: Lyon, France Completion Year: 2003

Photos: © Annie Ypperciel, Claude Cormier Architectes Paysagistes

As though they were hanging tapestries, thousands of silk flowers were used here to decorate a series of tree trunks as part of the French Summer Garden Festival. The artificial nature of the flowers reflects the constructive nature of landscape, while the silk refers to the importance of the textile industry in Lyon.

Tausende von Seidenblumen bedecken wie ein Wandteppich die Stämme einiger Bäume in der Anlage des French Summer Garden Festivals. Die Künstlichkeit dieser Blumen spiegelt wider, dass es sich um eine konstruierte Landschaft handelt, während sich das Material der Blumen, Seide, auf die Bedeutung der Textilindustrie in Lyon bezieht.

Des milliers de fleurs de soie recouvrent, ainsi un tapis, les troncs de quelques arbres dans l'enceinte du French Summer Garden Festival. L'artificialité des fleurs reflète sa nature constructive du paysage, alors que la soie fait référence à l'importance de l'industrie textile de la ville de Lyon.

Miles de flores de seda recubren, como si se tratase de un tapiz, los troncos de unos árboles en el recinto del French Summer Garden Festival. Lo artificial de las flores refleja la naturaleza constructiva del paisaje, mientras que la seda hace referencia a la importancia de la industria textil de Lyon.

Migliaia di fiori di seta ricoprono, come se si trattasse di un arazzo, alcuni tronchi d'alberi nel recinto del French Summer Garden Festival. L'artificialità dei fiori rispecchia la natura costruttiva del paesaggio, mentre la seta fa riferimento all'importanza dell'industria tessile di Lione.

Architecture Workshop
T: +81 3 54 49 83 37
F: +81 3 54 49 48 22
aws@archws.com
www.archws.com

ASPECT Landscape Architecture
Studio 61, 6, Marlborough Street, Surry Hills,
NSW 2010, Australia
T: +61 2 96 99 71 82
F: +61 2 96 99 71 92
aspectsydney@aspect.net.au
www.aspect.net.au

Atelier 4D
77, Avenue Albert 1er, 5000 Namur, Belgium
T: +32 81 21 48 20
F: +32 81 21 43 94
info@atelier4d.be
www.atelier4d.be

Birk Nielsens Tegnestue
Søndergade 1ª, 8000 Århus, Denmark
T: +45 86 20 21 10
F: +45 86 20 26 76
post@birknielsen.dk
www.birknielsen.dk

Carruthers Shaw and Partners Ltd.
2345 Yonge Street, Suite 200,
Toronto, Ontario M4P 2E5, Canada
T: +1 416 482 50 02
F: +1 416 482 50 40
cspa@csparch.com
www.csparch.com

Claude Cormier Architectes Paysagistes Inc.
5600 De Normanville, Montreal, Québec H2S 2B2, Canada
T: +1 514 849 82 62
F: +1 514 279 80 76
info@claudecormier.com
www.claudecormier.com

Dal Pian Arquitectos Associados
Av. Higienópolis 529 cj.11, 01238 001 Sâo Paulo, Brasil
T: +55 38 22 12 18
F: +55 38 22 51 86
dalpian@dalpian.arq.br
www.dalpian.arq.br

David Chipperfield
Cobham Mews, Agar Grove, Camden,
London NW1 9SB, United Kingdom
T: +44 20 72 67 94 22
F: +44 20 72 67 93 47
info@davidchipperfield.co.uk
www.davidchipperfield.com

EMBT Arquitectes Associats
Ptge. de la Pau, 10 Bis Pral., 08002 Barcelona, Spain
T: +34 93 412 53 42
F: +34 93 412 37 18
publicacio@mirallestagliabue.com
www.mirallestagliabue.com

Fauteux et Associés
3981 Boulevard Saint-Laurent, atelier 502,
Montreal, Québec H2W 1Y5, Canada
T: +1 514 842 55 53
F: +1 514 844 24 88
info@fauteux.ca
www.fauteux.ca

Foreign Office Architects
55 Curtain Road, London EC2A 3PT, United Kingdom
T: +44 20 70 33 98 00
F: +44 20 70 33 98 01
mail@f-o-a.net
www.f-o-a.net

Germán del Sol
Camino las Flores 11441, Las Condes, Santiago, Chile
T: +56 2 214 12 14
F: +56 2 214 11 47
contacto@entelchile.net
www.germandelsol.cl

Gustafson Guthrie Nichol Ltd.
Pier 55, Floor 3, 1101 Alaskan Way, Seattle, WA 98101, USA
T: +1 206 903 68 02
F: +1 206 903 68 04
contact@ggnltd.com
www.ggnltd.com

Hideki Yoshimatsu + Archipro Architects
3-6-16 104 Kitazawa Setagaya, Tokyo 155-0031, Japan
T: +81 3 54 53 50 81
F: +81 3 54 53 50 82
archipro@bd6.so-net.ne.jp
www.archipro.net

Isthmus Group Inc.
43 Sale Street, Freemans Bay, P.O. Box 90 366,
Auckland, Australia
T: +64 9 309 94 42
F: +64 9 309 90 60
akl@isthmus.co.nz
www.isthmus.co.nz

Janet Rosenberg & Associates
148 Kenwood Avenue, Toronto, Ontario M6C 2S3, Canada
T: +1 416 656 66 65
F: +1 416 656 57 56
office@jrala.ca
www.jrala.ca

Jean-Michel Landecy
22 Terreaux du Temple, 1201 Genève, Switzerland
T: +41 22 738 61 38
F: +41 22 738 61 39
info@jeanmichellandecy.com
www.jeanmichellandecy.com

Karres en Brands
Rigelstraat 55, 1223 AR Hilversum, Netherlands
T: +31 35 642 29 62
F: +31 35 683 63 62
info@karresenbrands.nl

Kengo Kuma & Associates
2-24-8 BY-CUBE 2-4F, Minamiaoyama, Minato-ku,
Tokyo 107-0062, Japan
T: +81 3 34 01 77 21
F: +81 3 34 01 76 73
kuma@ba2.so-net.jp
www.kkaa.co.jp

LAND-I
land-i@archicolture.com
www.archicolture.com

Landslag
Skölavörðustíg 11, 101 Reykjavik, Iceland
T: +354 535 53 00
F: +354 535 53 01
landslag@landslag.is
www.landslag.is

Landworks Studio
10 Derby Square, Salem, MA 01970, USA
T: +1 978 745 71 81
F: +1 978 740 28 23
mblier@ landworks-studio.com
www.landworks-studio.com

Levin Monsigny Landschaftsarchitekten GmbH
Schönhauser Allee 182, 10119 Berlin, Germany
T: +49 30 44 05 31 84
T: +49 30 44 05 36 51
mail@levin-monsigny.com
www.levin-monsigny.com

mcgregor & partners
21C Whistler Street, Manly,
NSW 2095, Australia
T: +61 2 99 77 38 53
F: +61 2 99 76 55 01
sydney@mcgregorpartners.com.au
www.mcgregorpartners.com.au

Mosbach Paysagistes
70 Quater Allee Darius Milhaud,
75019 Paris, France
T: +33 1 53 38 49 99
F: +33 1 42 41 22 10
mosbach.pays@wanadoo.fr

Nande Korpnik
300, Trubarjeva 3, Celje, Slovenia
T: +386 33 4926 086
korpnik@siol.net

NIP paysage
7468 Drolet, Montreal, Québec H2R SC4, Canada
T: +1 514 272 66 26
F: +1 514 272 66 26
nip@nippaysage.ca
www.nippaysage.ca

NO.MAD Arquitectos S.L.
Pez 27, 1° izq., oficina 2, 28004 Madrid, Spain
T: +34 91 532 70 34
F: +34 91 532 70 34
nomad@nomad.as
www.nomad.as

Obras architectes
42 rue d'Avron, 75020 Paris, France
T: +33 1 43 48 06 92
F: +33 1 43 70 24 30
obras@paysages.net
www.paysages.net

oslund.and.assoc.
115 Washington Avenue North,
Minneapolis, MN 55401, USA
T: +1 612 359 91 44
F: +1 612 359 96 25
toslund@oaala.com
www.oaala.com

Paolo L. Bürgi
6528 Camorino, Switzerland
T: +41 91 857 27 29
F: +41 91 857 36 26
burgi@burgi.ch
www.burgi.ch

Pere Joan Ravetllat & Carme Ribas Arquitectos
Rambla Catalunya 11, Prpal. 2ª,
Barcelona 08007, Spain
T: +93 280 26 90
F: +93 280 04 34
rqr@coac.net

Peter Walker and Partners
739 Allston Way, Berkeley, CA 94710, USA
T: +1 510 849 94 94
F: +1 510 849 93 33
berkeley@pwpla.com
www.pwpla.com

Pierre Lafon
29, rue Saint-Melaine, 35000 Rennes, France
T: +33 2 99 36 26 63
F: +33 2 99 63 71 86
pierlafon.archi@wanadoo.fr
www.pierlafon.net

Raderschall Landschaftsarchitekten
Burgstrasse 69, 8706 Meilen, Switzerland
T: +41 44 925 55 00
F: +41 44 925 55 01
info@raderschall.ch
www.raderschall.ch

RCR Arquitectes
Passeig Blay 34, 2, 17800 Olot, Spain
T: +34 972 26 91 05
F: +34 972 26 75 58
rcr.arquitectes@coac.es
www.rcrarquitectes.es

Rosa Grena Kliass
Rua Jesuíno de Arruda 888/131,
04532-082, São Paulo, SP, Brazil
T: +55 30 64 86 76
rgkliass@uol.com.br

Rotzler Krebs Partner GmbH
Lagerplatz 21, 8400 Winterthur, Switzerland
T: +41 52 269 08 60
F: +41 52 269 08 61
info@rkp.ch
www.rkp.ch

Sasaki Associates
64 Pleasant Street, Watertown, MA 02472, USA
T: +1 617 926 33 00
F: +1 617 924 27 48
tgray-pearce@sasaki.com
www.sasaki.com

Scapelab
Levstikov trg 4ª, Ljubljana 1000, Slovenia
T: +386 1 200 35 91
F: +386 1 200 35 98
info@scapelab.com
www.scapelab.com

SLA Landskabsarkitekter/Stig L. Andersson
Refshalevej A 153, Copenhagen 1432, Denmark
T: +45 33 91 13 16
F: +45 33 91 18 16
landskab@sla.dk
www.sla.dk

StoA Architecture
27, rue Vacon, 13001 Marseille, France
T: +33 4 9133 16 71
F: +33 4 9154 78 97
stoa@wanadoo.fr

Studio 3LHD
Varsavska 8/1, Zagreb 10000, Croatia
info@studio3lhd.hr
www.studio3lhd.hr

SWECO FFNS Architects
PO Box 17920, 11895 Stockholm, Sweden
T: +46 8 522 952 00
info@sweco.se
www.sweco.se/ffns

Taylor Cullity Lethlean
14–18 Holtom Street East,
Carlton, North, VIC 3054, Australia
perry.l@tcl.net.au
www.tcl.net.au

Turenscape
Bejing Turen Design Institute, 1st Floor,
Zhongguancun Fazhan Dasha, 12 Shangdi Xinxi Lu,
Haidian District, Beijing 100085, China
T: +86 10 62 96 74 08
F: +86 10 62 96 74 08
info@turenscape.com
www.turenscape.com

West 8
Wilhelminakade 68, P.O. Box 24326,
Rótterdam 3007, Netherlands
T: +31 10 485 58 01
F: +31 10 485 63 23
west8@west8.nl
www.west8.nl

Wraight & Associates Ltd.
Level 2, 282 Wakefield Street,
Wellington Aotearoa, New Zeland
T: +64 4 381 33 55
F: +64 4 381 33 66
office@waal.co.nz
www.waal.co.nz